Lift Every Voice and Sing

A Collection of Afro-American Spirituals and Other Songs

D1714168

The Church Hymnal Corporation
800 Second Avenue, New York NY 10017

The Church Pension Fund
800 Second Avenue
New York, NY 10017

ISBN: 0-89869-098-6

Table of Contents

Children's Hymns

25   *Jesus Loves the Little Children*
26   *Jesus Loves Me, This I Know*

Church Year—General

27   *Advent Tells Us Christ is Near*
28   Amen

Church Year—Christmas

29   Go Tell It on the Mountain
30   Some Children See Him
31   Rise Up, Shepherd, and Follow

Church Year—Passiontide

32   Jesu, Jesu, Fill Us with Your Love
33   Beneath the Cross of Jesus
34   He Never Said a Mumbling Word
35   *Jesus, Keep Me Near the Cross*
36   Rock of Ages
37   The Old Rugged Cross
38   Were You There
39   *When I Survey the Wondrous Cross*

Church Year—Easter

40   He Arose
41   *Am I a Soldier of the Cross*
42   Done Made My Vow
43   Down by the Riverside
44   Every Time I Feel the Spirit
45   O Holy Savior
46   I've Decided to Make Jesus My Choice
47   Just As I Am
48   *My Faith Looks Up to Thee*

Community

Faith

Mission

Prayer

Sacraments—Baptism

Sacraments—Eucharist

Sacraments—Ordination

Social Justice

Witness

Liturgical

PREFACE

It has taken a long time for spirituals to gain acceptance in the Episcopal Church. Even with the publishing of this supplement to the Church Hymnal, there will be many who still question its appropriateness. All forms of folk art have difficulty being accepted at their first flowering; and in those churches having a stated liturgy it has been all but impossible to gain admission. In these later years, with the great surge of interest in racial, as well as genealogical, origins, it is not surprising that this music has taken its place as a source of pride and inspiration. What was once regarded as a product of a slave mentality is now appreciated as a mark of racial genius. What was once dismissed as hardly worthy of liturgical notice is now evaluated as artistry that compares favorably, musically and emotionally, with the greatest music within the Christian tradition. It is agreed among students of the spirituals that, like all true folksongs, they were originally intended for group singing. There are certainly individuals who have achieved the highest form of expression in their rendition of the spirituals, but it is the group, the congregation, that has saved this music from becoming either the sentimental ballad or the rhythmic secular dance tune. The spirituals are the possession of no one denomination, but are the expression of the overpowering faith of all Black Christians. Within the Episcopal Church, it is the hope of the editors, the Commission for Black Ministries, that there will be acceptance far beyond those parishes composed largely of Black people. This music will serve the whole Church well, if, in making it its own, it will come to understand something more of the mission of all people in today's world.

The inclusion of many of the so-called "evangelistic hymns" is a simple recognition of the important part they also have played in the Black religious experience. Just as the slaves not only adopted the religion of their masters, but transformed it into a Gospel that had particular meaning for themselves, so the Black Christians have taken the hymnody of the evangelical church and claimed it for their own. These hymns do not have the theological purity of the spirituals, nor do they arise out of the bitter experience of Black people. In adopting this music, again like the Christian religion itself, the Black congregation has used the notation merely as a guide. The free expression of enthusiastic faith has raised this music into a genre that rightly takes its place within Black congregational worship.

The spirituals and the evangelistic hymns together stand as a witness that Black Episcopalians need not desert their grand musical heritage. They bring this as a rich gift to be included within the older Anglican tradition. In so doing, they, along with other races, nationalities and ethnic groups who have accepted Jesus Christ as Lord, make their own rightful contribution to the catholicity of the Church, and continue the apostolic injunction to sing "with grace in your hearts to the Lord."

The Rt. Rev. John M. Burgess
Retired Bishop of Massachusetts

INTRODUCTION

The Commission for Black Ministries of the Executive Council of the Episcopal Church commends this Hymnal *Lift Every Voice and Sing* to the Episcopal Church for use alongside of the official Hymnal. It is hoped that this collection of spirituals and other songs will further enrich the worship services and Liturgy in all of our congregations. We also hope that Blacks in other predominantly white denominations and churches will find this Hymnal valuable in their worship services.

This Hymnal Project was conceived by the Rev. Franklin D. Turner, National Staff Officer for Black Ministries, for the Episcopal Church. It was developed in response to the Theological Statement of the Episcopal Commission for Black Ministries of the Executive Council. The Statement says in part that "our theological perspective must be drawn not only from the tradition of our Church, but also from the culture of our people" and "that we need to develop an Afro-American Hymnal that draws heavily on the wealth of Negro spirituals and gospel music. That we actively encourage liturgical enrichment that enhances our worship life." We hope this hymnal will in fact do the above.

For a more detailed history of the music practices in Black Episcopal Churches see the article in the appendix by Dr. Irene V. Jackson, who served as Consultant and researcher for the hymnal project.

Now something about the background of Afro-American religious music. All Afro-American music had a difficult time gaining respect as an authentic contribution to American culture. Religious music was no exception.

As late as 1893, a European anthropologist attempted to discount the originality of the spirituals and wrote that "the spiritual was not a Negro original but imitative of the white hymns, gospel songs and folk songs with which the Negro was surrounded."

An American professor wrote a sizeable book in 1933 echoing the same point of view. He contended that the Negro spirituals were derivative of white spirituals and gospel songs. He proved that some Negro spirituals were similar to white songs, but failed to take into account factors other than verse similarity, such as the music form of the spirituals. Nearly all the Negro spirituals employ the African "call and response" chant form which is uniquely African. More importantly, he missed the theology contained in the spirituals: the theology of liberation and hope.

Be that as it may, the Fisk Jubilee Singers' historic American and European concert tours, extending from 1871 to 1878, firmly heralded the Negro spirituals as a new and authentic contribution to the world. Today there is not an area of American music unaffected by Afro-American music, whether acknowledged or denied.

Over the past two decades, Afro-American religious music has been widely imitated and validated time and time again. Unfortunately, Afro-Americans, particularly those in predominantly white churches, have not felt comfortable using their own music in formal church services, but instead relegated this music to use at civic and social gatherings. Although Black Episcopalians could not or would not use spirituals in their formal worship, they constantly hummed and sang these songs in private. The spirituals are a part of the life and blood of Black People.

However, with the civil rights, Black awareness, and liturgical movements of the 1950s and 60s, Black Americans gained courage to boldly proclaim and affirm their religious heritage, including their music. The liturgical movement of the church was intended to more closely relate worship to the cultural experiences of the people. Hence the experiment with folk, jazz, and soul masses. Even before the liturgical movement, some priests and congregations experimented with indigenizing the liturgy to the church by incorporating Negro spirituals. This practice was not widespread because it was not encouraged and was thought to be unacceptable, inappropriate, and "not Episcopal". Some said that spirituals could not fit into the Episcopal Liturgy. Thank God that kind of thinking is hopefully vanishing.

Moreover, we believe that every people has the right to worship God in their own language and culture. The spirituals are an integral part of Black culture and therefore must be an integral part of worship, no matter what the denomination.

America is rich in its cultural heritage because she embodies strands of every culture on the face of the earth. Blacks too have benefited from this cultural pluralism, and have appropriated many of the hymns and songs of other church traditions for their own, as is seen in this supplement.

With the intensive search today for new music and new ways to enrich church services, this supplemental hymnal is an offering to the Episcopal Church. Most of the music is not new, but old and tested. It helped to sustain a people through a most dismal period of their history. What will be new is its widespread use in the worship of the church.

This supplement should not be perceived as a replacement for the *1940 Hymnal* or the creation of a separate hymnal for Black Episcopalians. Rather, it is designed to serve as a supplementary or a complementary hymnal.

The selections contained in this supplement are in no way exhaustive of the Black religious music tradition, but include many of the best loved and familiar spirituals and other songs used in traditional Black worship. Many of the themes of the spirituals focus on personal assurance, comfort, and hope rather than the broad scope of theological and biblical motifs of the church year.

This is understandable because these songs emanated from the life and experiences of an oppressed and enslaved people. Nonetheless, many of these songs are quite appropriate for various sacramental rites and services, and can also be used throughout the church year. The *1940 Hymnal* will continue to be used for the specific liturgical observances.

A matter which should be brought to our attention is the use of the pronoun "I" in many of the spirituals, as in "Lord I'm Coming Home"; "Lord I Want to be a Christian in My Heart," etc. It must be remembered that African slaves were stripped of nearly all human dignity and were looked upon as mere property, and they had to constantly remind themselves of their "somebodiness," especially in the sight of God. Also, the African slave came to America with a strong sense of tribe, community, and nation, and the "I" so commonly used in the spirituals does not refer to the individual "I", but rather the corporate "I" which points to the person's connectedness with the community. The "call and response" chant form is a good illustration of this. The soloist will sing, for example, "Lord I Want to be a Christian," and the people will answer "in my heart". The history of the spirituals demonstrates that they are not the product of the individual, but a community effort.

To further enforce the concept of corporateness in worship, these spirituals and other songs in this supplement were selected primarily for congregational singing and not intended for individual or choir performances.

So, we hope that everybody will "Lift Every Voice and Sing".

The Rev. Franklin D. Turner, D.D.
Staff Officer for Black Ministries
Episcopal Church Center
815 Second Avenue
New York, New York 10017

COMMENTS ON THE SELECTIONS

Lift Every Voice and Sing grows out of an extensive search of existing Afro-American song literature. This was a formidable task, since most of the spirituals and contemporary spirituals known as gospels, which form a large part of this hymnal, were not readily accessible. Most of the songs were contained in collections which were out-of-print and available only in archives and repositories such as the Schomburg Center for Research in Black Culture and the Library of Congress.

In addition to the search for and compilation of songs, an important aspect of this project was the research that culminated in an essay, "Music Among Blacks in the Episcopal Church: Some Preliminary Considerations." This essay establishes an historical framework for this hymnal.

This collection brings together an important body of Afro-American sacred songs and thus celebrates the creative spirit of those "unknown bards" who first gave utterance to songs that are a significant part of America's religious song heritage. This hymnal, also, calls attention to little known composers, song writers, and arrangers who crafted these folk song gems and gave them new form. Many of the composers and arrangers in this collection are seminal figures in Afro-American music history; however they are generally unknown. Afro-Americans who come to mind in this regard are Edward Boatner, Harry T. Burleigh, R. Nathaniel Dett, Carl Diton, Charles A.Tindley, John Wesley Work, Clarence C. White, among several others who are represented in this hymnal. These individuals have left a rich musical legacy.

In the preparation of *Lift Every Voice and Sing*, songs were selected for their effectiveness as congregational songs and for the ease by which they could be learned and sung by the average person in the pew.

This hymnal stands apart from others. It contains arrangements of traditional songs from the Afro-American heritage for congregational rather than choir use. Because spirituals are most familiar as anthem arrangements, users are advised that the arrangements here are, by necessity, less ambitious than the arrangements which are more familiar.

In the actual performance of the songs, unison or part-singing is encouraged, as well as improvisation, where appropriate. Many of the songs stem from an oral or folk tradition where textual and melodic interpolation is part of the accepted performance practice. Thus, individual congregations should add or modify texts as they see fit. This is especially true in the singing of spirituals where verses are not prescribed or standardized.

Songs can be sung with or without instrumental accompaniment. When instrumental accompaniment is used, organists or pianists are encouraged to improvise in a manner that preserves the integrity of the genre, as well as the arranger's or composer's work. In the folk tradition — in which these songs are largely based — improvisation is encouraged, particularly in the performance of gospels where the score is a blueprint for performance.

Every effort was given to fully acknowledge every text and tune. Instances where songs are part of folk or oral tradition, the designation of "traditional," for example, is assigned to the left, below the score where text details are given. Below the score on the right, details are given about the genre, tune source, arranger, or composer. These details were culled from research and are based on a knowledge of the Afro-American religious song tradition.

Irene V. Jackson, Ph.D.
Compiler and General Editor

ACKNOWLEDGMENTS

This project began in 1978 under the aegis of the Office of Black Ministries when a commitment was made to publish a hymnal that would reflect the religious musical heritage of Afro-Americans.

This present work was a collective effort; many individuals contributed in both tangible and intangible ways. Foremost, all the "unsung" composers and arrangers who are represented in this hymnal must be acknowledged. Professor Evelyn D. White of Howard University, Dr. Horace C. Boyer of the University of Massachusetts, Amherst and Mr. Richard Smallwood, founder and director of Richard Smallwood Singers of Washington, D.C. are to be cited for their contributions. Mr. David Hurd of General Theological Seminary, and Mr. Hale Smith, composer, were helpful in lending their expertise. Mr. Frank Hemlin and Mrs. Joyce Glover of The Church Hymnal Corporation provided technical assistance and must be acknowledged. Also, appreciation extends to the Rev. Drs. Carlton Hayden and Robert Bennett for their scholarly research that was invaluable in reconstructing the history of the musical activities of Black Episcopalians.

This hymnal was reviewed at various stages of its preparation by clergy, lay persons, and church musicians. Members of this committee included the Rev. Dr. Robert Bennett, the Rt. Rev. John M. Burgess, Dr. Owilender Grant, the Rev. Dr. Carlton Hayden, Mrs. Ruth Horton, the Rev. William J. Walker, the Rev. Dr. Orris G. Walker, and the Rev. Dr. Frederick B. Williams.

Thanks are due, also, to the many individuals who have patiently awaited the publication of this hymnal. Your support was appreciated.

Irene V. Jackson, Ph.D.
Franklin D. Turner, D.D.

1   Come to Me

1. "Come to Me, Ye who are hard op - prest;
2. "Come to Me!" Je - ho - vah gen - tly pleads;

1. Lay your head gen - tly up - on my breast; _____
2. "Come to Me I can sup-ply all needs; _____

1. Come to Me, _____ And I will give you
2. And My way _____ Un - to green pas - ture

1. rest; Wea - ry one, Hith - er come! God is your home!"
2. leads; Free from sin! En - ter in! God is your home!"

Traditional

Spiritual
Arr. R. Nathaniel Dett

ASSURANCE

2   Blessed Assurance

1. Bless-ed as - sur - ance, Je - sus is mine! O what a
2. Per - fect sub - mis - sion, per-fect de - light, Vi-sions of
3. Per - fect sub - mis - sion, all is at rest, I in my

1. fore-taste of glo - ry di - vine! Heir of sal - va - tion, pur-chase of
2. rap - ture now burst on my sight; An-gels de - scend - ing, bring from a -
3. Sav - ior am hap-py and blest; Watch-ing and wait - ing, look-ing a -

1. God, Born of His Spir - it, washed in His blood.
2. bove Ech - oes of mer - cy, whis - pers of love.
3. bove, Filled with His good - ness, lost in His love.

Fanny Crosby

Hymn
Phoebe P. Knapp

ASSURANCE

Refrain

This is my sto - ry, this is my song, Prais - ing my Sav - ior all the day long; This is my sto - ry, this is my song, Prais - ing my Sav - ior all the day long.

ASSURANCE

3　His Eye Is on the Sparrow

Why should I feel dis - cour - aged, __ Why should the shad-ows come, __ Why should my heart be lone - ly, __ And long for heav'n and home, __ When Je - sus is __ my por - tion? __ My con-stant friend is He: __ His eye is on __ the spar-row, __ And I know He watch-es me; __ His

Mrs. C. D. Martin

Spiritual
Charles H. Gabriel
Arr. Horace Clarence Boyer

ASSURANCE

eye is on the spar-row,___ and I know He watch-es me.___ I

Refrain

sing be-cause I'm hap-py,___ I sing be-cause I'm free; For His

eye is on the spar-row,___ And I know He watch-es me.___

2. "Let not your heart be troubled," His tender word I hear,
   And resting on His goodness, I lose my doubts and fears,
   Tho' by the path He leadeth, But one step I may see:
   His eye is on the sparrow, And I know He watches me;
   His eye is on the sparrow, And I know He watches me.

3. Whenever I am tempted, Whenever clouds arise,
   When songs give place to sighing, When hope within me dies,
   I draw the closer to Him; From care He sets me free;
   His eye is on the sparrow, And I know He watches me;
   His eye is on the sparrow, And I know He watches me.

ASSURANCE

4   I Must Tell Jesus

1. I must tell Je - sus all of my tri - als; I can - not
2. I must tell Je - sus all of my trou - bles, He is a
3. Tempt-ed and tried I need a great Sav - ior, One who can
4. O how the world to e - vil al - lures me! O how my

1. bear these bur-dens a - lone, In my dis - tress He kind-ly will
2. kind, com - pas-sion-ate Friend; If I but ask Him, He will de -
3. help my bur-dens to bear; I must tell Je - sus, I must tell
4. heart is tempt-ed to sin! I must tell Je - sus, and He will

1. help me, He ev - er loves and cares for His own.
2. liv - er, Makes of my trou - bles quick - ly an end.
3. Je - sus; He all my cares and sor - rows will share.
4. help me O - ver the world the vic - t'ry to win.

Elisha A. Hoffman

Hymn
Elisha A. Hoffman

ASSURANCE

Refrain

I must tell Je - sus! I must tell Je - sus! I can-not bear my bur-dens a - lone; I must tell Je - sus! I must tell Je - sus! Je - sus can help me, Je - sus a - lone.

ASSURANCE

5 God Will Take Care of You

1. Be not dis-may-ed what-e'er be-tide, God will take care of you;
2. Thro' days of toil when heart doth fail, God will take care of you;
3. All you may need He will pro-vide, God will take care of you;
4. No mat-ter what may be the test, God will take care of you;

1. Be-neath His wings of love a-bide, God will take care of you.
2. When dan-gers fierce your path as-sail, God will take care of you.
3. Noth-ing you ask will be de-nied, God will take care of you.
4. Lean, wea-ry one, up-on His breast, God will take care of you.

Refrain

God will take care of you, Thro' ev-'ry day, O'er all the way;

He will take care of you, God will take care of you.
take care of you.

C. D. Martin

Gospel
W. S. Martin

ASSURANCE

6 I'm So Glad Jesus Lifted Me

1. I'm __ so __ glad, __ Je - sus lift - ed me,
2. Sa - tan had me bound, __ Je - sus lift - ed me,
3. When I was in trou - ble, Sing - ing

Glo - ry Hal - le - lu - jah! Je - sus lift - ed me.

Traditional

Spiritual
Arr. Richard Smallwood

ASSURANCE

7 Lead Me, Guide Me

Refrain

Lead me, guide me, a - long the way,

For _ if you lead me, I can - not stray.

Lord, _ let me walk each day with thee.

Lead me, Oh Lord, lead me. _

Doris M. Akers

Gospel
Doris M. Akers
Arr. Richard Smallwood

ASSURANCE

1. I am weak and I need thy strength and power to
2. Help me tread in the paths of right-eous-ness, Be my
3. I am lost if you take your hand from me, I am

1. help me o-ver my weak-est hour. Help me
2. aid when Sa-tan and sin op-press. I am
3. blind with-out thy Light to see, Lord, just

1. through the dark-ness thy face to see,
2. put-ting all my trust in thee.
3. al-ways let me thy ser-vant be.

1. Lead me, Oh Lord, lead me.
2. Lead me, Oh Lord, lead me.
3. Lead me, Oh Lord, lead me.

ASSURANCE

8 Jesus, Lover of My Soul

1. Je - sus, Lov - er of my soul, Let me to Thy bo - som fly,
2. Oth - er ref - uge have I none, Hangs my help-less soul on Thee;
3. Plen-teous grace with Thee is found, Grace to cleanse from ev - 'ry sin;

1. While the near - er wa - ters roll, While the tem-pest still is high:
2. Leave, ah! leave me not a - lone, Still sup-port and com - fort me!
3. Let the heal - ing streams a - bound, Make and keep me pure with-in.

1. Hide me, O my Sav - ior, hide, Till the storm of life be past;
2. All my trust on Thee is stayed; All my help from Thee I bring;
3. Thou of life the foun - tain art, Free - ly let me take of Thee:

1. Safe in - to the ha - ven guide, O re-ceive my soul at last.
2. Cov - er my de - fence - less head With the sha - dow of Thy wing.
3. Spring Thou up with - in my heart, Rise to all e - ter - ni - ty. A - men.

Charles Wesley

Hymn
Simeon B. Marsh

ASSURANCE

sink - ing sand, All oth - er ground is sink - ing sand. A - men.

11   O Master, Let Me Walk with Thee

1. O Mas - ter, let me walk with Thee In low - ly
2. Help me the slow of heart to move By some clear,
3. Teach me Thy pa - tience; still with Thee In clos - er,
4. In hope that sends a shin - ing ray Far down the

1. paths of serv - ice free; Tell me Thy se - cret;
2. win - ning word of love; Teach me the way - ward
3. dear - er com - pa - ny. In work that keeps faith
4. fu - ture's broad - 'ning way, In peace that on - ly

1. help me bear The strain of toil, the fret of care.
2. feet to stay, And guide them in the home - ward way.
3. sweet and strong, In trust that tri - umphs o - ver wrong.
4. Thou canst give, With Thee, O Mas - ter, let me live.

Washington Gladden

Hymn
H. Percy Smith

ASSURANCE

12   Take My Hand, Precious Lord

1. Pre - cious Lord, take my hand, Lead me on, let me
2. When my way grows drear, pre - cious Lord, lin - ger
3. When the dark - ness ap - pears and the night draws

1. stand, I am tired, I am weak, I am worn;
2. near, When my life is al - most gone,
3. near, And the day is past and gone,

1. Thru the storm, thru the night, Lead me on to the
2. Hear my cry, hear my call, Hold my hand lest I
3. At the riv - er I stand, Guide my feet, hold my

Thomas A. Dorsey

Gospel
Thomas A. Dorsey
Arr. Richard Smallwood

ASSURANCE

1. light,
2. fall;   Take my hand, pre-cious Lord,   Lead me home.
3. hand,

13   Guide Me, O Thou Great Jehovah

1. Guide me, O thou great Je - ho - vah, Pil - grim through this
2. O - pen now the crys - tal foun-tains Whence the liv - ing
3. Feed me with the heav'n - ly man - na In this bar - ren
4. When I tread the verge of Jor - dan, Bid my anx - ious

1. bar - ren land;   I   am weak, but   thou art might - y;
2. wa - ters flow;   Let   the fier - y,   cloud - y pil - lar
3. wil - der - ness;   Be   my sword, and   shield, and ban - ner,
4. fears sub - side;   Death   of death, and   hell's de - struc - tion,

1. Hold   me   with   thy   power - ful   hand.
2. Lead   me   all   my   jour - ney   through.
3. Be   the   Lord   my   Right - eous - ness.
4. Land   me   safe   on   Ca - naan's   side.   A - men.

William Williams
Tr. Peter Williams

Hymn
John B. Dykes

ASSURANCE

14   There Is a Balm in Gilead

There is a Balm in Gil-e-ad, To make the wound-ed whole, There is a Balm in Gil-e-ad, To heal the sin-sick soul. There is a soul.

Some-times I feel dis-cour-aged, And think my work's in vain, But then the Ho-ly Spir-it Re-vives my soul a-gain.

Traditional

Spiritual
Arr. R. Nathaniel Dett

ASSURANCE

2. Don't ever be discouraged
   For Jesus is your friend,
   And if you lack for knowledge,
   He'll ne'er refuse to lend.

3. If you cannot preach like Peter,
   If you cannot pray like Paul,
   You can tell the love of Jesus,
   You can say, "He died for all."

15 Now the Day Is Over

1. Now the day is o - ver,
2. Je - sus, give the wea - ry
3. Grant to lit - tle chil - dren
4. Com - fort ev - 'ry suf - f'rer
5. Thro' the long night - watch - es
6. When the morn - ing wak - ens,

1. Night is draw - ing nigh,
2. Calm and sweet re - pose;
3. Vis - ions bright of Thee;
4. Watch - ing late in pain;
5. May Thine an - gels spread
6. Then may I a - rise

Shad - ows of the
With Thy tend - 'rest
Guard the sail - ors,
Those who plan some
Their white wings a -
Pure, and fresh, and

1. ev - 'ning Steal a - cross the sky.
2. bless - ing May mine eye - lids close.
3. toss - ing On the deep blue sea.
4. e - vil From their sin re - strain.
5. bove me, Watch - ing round my bed.
6. sin - less, In Thy ho - ly eyes. A - men.

1. ev - 'ning steal a - cross the sky.

Sabine Baring-Gould

Hymn
Sabine Baring-Gould

ASSURANCE

16　Through It All

1. I've had man-y tears and sor-rows, I've had ques-tions for
2. I've been to lots of plac - es, And I've seen a lot
3. I thank God for the moun-tains, And I thank Him for

1. to - mor - row, There've been times I did-n't know right from
2. of fac - es, There've been times I felt so all a -
3. the val - leys, I thank Him for the storms He brought me

1. wrong; But in ev - ery sit - u -
2. lone; But in my lone - ly
3. through; For if I'd nev - er

1. a - tion God gave bless - ed con - so - la - tion That my
2. hours, Yes, those pre - cious lone - ly hours, Je - sus
3. had a prob-lem I would-n't know that He could solve them, I'd

Andrae Crouch

Gospel
Melody, Andrae Crouch
Arr. Horace Clarence Boyer

ASSURANCE

1. tri - als come to on - ly make me strong.
2. let me know that I was His own.
3. nev - er know what faith in God could do.

Through it all, Through it all, I've learned to trust in

Je - sus, I've learned to trust in God; Through it all,

Through it all, I've learned to de - pend up - on His Word.

ASSURANCE

17 I Want Jesus to Walk with Me

Refrain

I want Je - sus to walk with me, (walk with me,) I want
Je - sus to walk with me; (with me;) All a - long my pil - grim
jour - ney, I want Je - sus to walk with me.

1. In my tri - als, walk with me, walk with me, In my
2. In my sor - rows, walk with me, walk with me, In my
3. In my trou - bles, walk with me, walk with me, In my
Lord,

Traditional

Spiritual
Arr. Edward C. Deas

ASSURANCE

1. tri - als,   walk with   me, walk with me, When the shades of   life   are
2. sor - rows,   walk with   me, walk with me, When my heart with - in   is
3. trou - bles,   walk with   me, walk with me, When my life   be - comes a

Lord,

1. fall - ing,   Lord, I want   Je - sus   to walk with   me.
2. ach - ing,   Lord, I want   Je - sus   to walk with   me.
3. bur - den,   Lord, I want   Je - sus   to walk with   me.

ASSURANCE

18   We'll Understand It Better By and By

1. We are tossed and driv-en on the rest - less sea of time; Som-bre skies and howl-ing temp-est oft suc-ceeds. a bright sun-shine; In that land of per-fect day, when the mists have rolled a-way, We will un-der-stand it bet-ter by and by.

2. We are oft - en des - ti - tute of the things that life de-mands, Want of shel - ter and of food thirst - y hills and bar - ren lands; We are trust - ing in the Lord, and ac-cord - ing to His word We will un-der-stand it bet-ter by and by.

3. Tri - als dark on ev - 'ry hand, and we can - not un - der-stand All the ways that God would lead us to that Bless - ed Prom - ised Land; But He guides us with His eye and we'll fol - low 'till we die, For we'll un-der-stand it bet-ter by and by.

4. Temp - ta - tions, hid - den snares, oft - en take us un - a -wares, And our hearts are made to bleed for a tho't - less word or deed, And we won - der why the test when we try to do our best; But we'll un-der-stand it bet-ter by and by.

C. A. Tindley

Gospel Hymn
C. A. Tindley
Arr. F. A. Clark

ASSURANCE

ASSURANCE

19 Abide with Me

1. A - bide with me: fast falls the e - ven - tide;
2. Swift to its close ebbs out life's lit - tle day;
3. I need Thy pres - ence ev - ery pas - sing hour;
4. I fear no foe, with Thee at hand to bless;
5. Hold Thou Thy cross be - fore my clos - ing eyes;

1. The dark - ness deep - ens; Lord, with me a - bide!
2. Earth's joys grow dim, its glo - ries pass a - way;
3. What but Thy grace can foil the tempt - er's power?
4. Ills have no weight, and tears no bit - ter - ness.
5. Shine through the gloom and point me to the skies:

1. When oth - er help - ers fail, and com - forts flee,
2. Change and de - cay in all a - round I see.
3. Who, like Thy - self, my guide and stay can be?
4. Where is death's sting? Where, grave, thy vic - to - ry?
5. Heav'n's morn - ing breaks, and earth's vain shad - ows flee;

1. Help of the help - less, O a - bide with me.
2. O Thou who chang - est not, a - bide with me.
3. Through cloud and sun - shine, Lord, a - bide with me.
4. I tri - umph still, if Thou a - bide with me.
5. In life, in death, O Lord, a - bide with me. A - men.

Henry F. Lyte

Hymn
William H. Monk

ASSURANCE/BURIAL

20 Come, Ye Disconsolate

1. Come, ye dis - con - so - late, wher - e'er ye lan - guish,
2. Joy of the des - o - late, light of the stray - ing,
3. Here see the Bread of life; see wa - ters flow - ing

1. Come to the mer - cy - seat, fer - vent - ly kneel:
2. Hope of the pen - i - tent, fade - less and pure!
3. Forth from the throne of God, pure from a - bove:

1. Here bring your wound - ed hearts, here tell your an - guish;
2. Here speaks the Com - fort - er, ten - der - ly say - ing,
3. Come to the feast of love; come, ev - er know - ing

1. Earth has no sor - row that heav'n can - not heal.
2. "Earth has no sor - row that heav'n can - not cure."
3. Earth has no sor - row but heav'n can re - move.

Thomas Moore,   Hymn
St. 3, Thomas Hastings   *Arr. Samuel Webbe*

ASSURANCE/BURIAL

21   He'll Understand and Say "Well Done"

1. If when you give the best of your serv-ice,
2. Mis-un-der-stood, the Sav-ior of sin-ners,
3. If when this life of la-bor is end-ed,
4. But if you try and fail in your try-ing

1. Tell-ing the world that the Sav-ior is come;
2. Hung on the cross; He was God's on-ly Son;
3. And the re-ward of the race you have run;
4. Hands sore and scarred from the work you've be-gun;

1. Be not dis-mayed when men don't be-lieve you;
2. Oh! hear Him call-ing His Fa-ther in Heav'n,
3. Oh! the sweet rest pre-pared for the faith-ful,
4. Take up your cross, run quick-ly to meet Him;

1. He un-der-stands; He'll say, "Well Done."
2. Not my will, but Thine be done."
3. Will be His blest and fi-nal "well done."
4. He'll un-der-stand He'll say "Well Done."

Lucie E. Campbell

Gospel
Lucie E. Campbell

ASSURANCE/BURIAL

Oh, when I come to the end of my jour - ney, Wea - ry of life and the bat - tle is won; Car - r'ing the staff and cross of Re-demp-tion, He'll un-der - stand, and say 'Well Done."

22 Nearer, My God, to Thee

1. Near - er, my God, to Thee, Near - er to Thee!
2. Though like the wan - der - er, The sun goes down,
3. There let the way ap - pear Steps un - to heav'n;
4. Then, with my wak - ing thoughts Bright with Thy praise,
5. Or if on joy - ful wing, Cleav - ing the sky,

1. E'en though it be a cross That rais - eth me;
2. Dark - ness be o - ver me, My rest a stone;
3. All that Thou send - est me In mer - cy giv'n;
4. Out of my ston - y griefs Beth - el I'll raise;
5. Sun, moon and stars for - got, Up - wards I fly,

Refrain

1. Still all my song would be,
2. Yet in my dreams I'd be
3. An - gels to beck - on me Near - er, my God, to Thee,
4. So by my woes to be
5. Still all my song shall be

Near - er my God, to Thee, Near - er to Thee. A - men.

Sarah Adams

Hymn
Lowell Mason

ASSURANCE/BURIAL

23   O God, Our Help in Ages Past

1. O God, our help in a - ges past, Our
2. Un - der the shad - ow of thy throne Thy
3. Be - fore the hills in or - der stood, Or
4. A thou - sand a - ges in thy sight Are
5. Time, like an ev - er - roll - ing stream, Bears
6. O God, our help in a - ges past, Our

1. hope for years to come, Our shel - ter from the
2. saints have dwelt se - cure; Suf - fi - cient is thine
3. earth re - ceived her frame, From ev - er - last - ing
4. like an eve - ning gone; Short as the watch that
5. all its sons a - way; They fly, for - got - ten,
6. hope for years to come, Be thou our guard while

1. storm - y blast, And our e - ter - nal home!
2. arm a - lone, And our de - fense is sure.
3. thou art God, To end - less years the same.
4. ends the night Be - fore the ris - ing sun.
5. as a dream Dies at the op - 'ning day.
6. life shall last, And our e - ter - nal home. A - men.

Isaac Watts

Hymn
William Croft

ASSURANCE/BURIAL

24 Swing Low, Sweet Chariot

Swing low, sweet char - i - ot,— Com-ing for to car - ry me home,

Swing low,— sweet char - i - ot,— com-ing for to car - ry me home.

1. I looked o - ver Jor - dan and what did I see,—
2. If you get— there be - fore— I do,—
3. I'm some - times— up, I'm— some - times down,—

Com-ing for to car - ry me home, A band— of an - gels
Com-ing for to car - ry me home, Tell all— my friends I'm
Com-ing for to car - ry me home, But still— my soul feels

Traditional   Spiritual

ASSURANCE/BURIAL

com - ing af - ter me,___ coming for to car - ry me home.
com - ing___ too,___ coming for to car - ry me home.
heav - en - ly___ bound,. coming for to car - ry me home.

*D. C. after
each stanza*

25   Jesus Loves the Little Children

Je - sus loves the lit - tle chil - dren, All the chil - dren of the

world.   Red and yel - low, black and white, They are pre-cious in His sight.

Je - sus loves the lit - tle chil - dren of the world.

Anonymous

Hymn
Traditional

CHILDREN'S HYMN

26   Jesus Loves Me, This I Know

1. Je - sus loves me! this I know, For the Bi - ble tells me so;
2. Je - sus loves me! He who died Heav-en's gate to o - pen wide;
3. Je - sus, take this heart of mine, Make it pure and whol-ly Thine;

1. Lit - tle ones to Him be - long, They are weak but He is strong.
2. He will wash a - way my sin, Let His lit - tle child come in.
3. On the cross You died for me. I will try to live for Thee.

Yes, Je - sus loves me! Yes, Je - sus loves me!

Yes, Je - sus loves me! The Bi - ble tells me so.

Anne B. Warner

Hymn
William B. Bradbury

CHILDREN'S HYMNS

27 Advent Tells Us Christ Is Near

1. Advent tells us Christ is near; Christ-mas tells us
2. Those three Sun-days be-fore Lent Will pre-pare us
3. Ho-ly Week and Eas-ter, then, Tell who died and
4. Yes, and Christ as-cend-ed, too, To pre-pare a
5. Then, He sent the Ho-ly Ghost, On the Day of
6. Last of all, we hum-bly sing Glo-ry to our

1. Christ is here! In E-pi-pha-ny we trace
2. to re-pent. That in Lent we may be-gin
3. rose a-gain: O that hap-py Eas-ter Day!
4. place for you; So we give Him spe-cial praise
5. Pen-te-cost, With us ev-er to a-bide:
6. God and King, Glo-ry to the One in Three,

1. All the glo-ry of His grace.
2. Earn-est-ly to mourn for sin.
3. "Christ is ris'n in-deed," we say.
4. Af-ter those great for-ty days.
5. Well may we keep Whit-sun-tide!
6. On the Feast of Trin-i-ty. A-men.

Katherine Hankey

Hymn
Wea Teba

CHURCH YEAR

28 Amen

A - men, A - men, A - men, A - men, A - men.

A -

1. See the lit - tle ba - by
2. See Him at the tem - ple
3. See Him in the gar - den
4. See Him on Cal - va - ry

Traditional

Spiritual
Arr. Richard Smallwood

CHURCH YEAR

men,   A - men,

1. Ly - ing in a man - ger   On   Christ - mas morn - ing.
2. Talk - ing to the el - ders   How they mar - veled at His wis - dom.
3. Pray - ing to His fa - ther   As   Ju - das be - trays Him.
4. Dy - ing for our sins   But He rose   on   East - er.

A -   men, A - men, A - men.

A -   men, A - men, A - men.

CHURCH YEAR

29   Go Tell It on the Mountain

Go tell it on the moun-tain, O-ver the hills and ev-'ry where;
Go tell it on the moun-tain, That Je-sus Christ is born.

1. When I was a seek-er, I sought both night and day, I
2. He made me a watch-man, up - on a cit - y wall, And

asked the Lord to help me, And He showed me the way. _____
if I am a Chris-tian, I am the least of all. _____

*Repeat Refrain
after each stanza*

Traditional   Spiritual

CHURCH YEAR — CHRISTMAS

30 Some Children See Him

1. Some chil-dren see Him lil - y white, The ba - by Je - sus born this night,
2. Some chil-dren see Him al-mond-eyed, This Sav-ior whom we kneel be-side,
3. The chil-dren in each dif-ferent place Will see the ba -by Je - sus' face

1. Some chil-dren see Him bronzed and brown. The Lord of heaven to earth come down;
2. Some chil-dren see Him dark as they, Sweet Mar - y's Son, to whom we pray;
3. O lay a - side each earth-ly thing, And with thy heart as of - fer - ing,

1. Some chil-dren see Him lil - y white, With tress - es soft and fair.
2. Some chil-dren see Him al - mond-eyed, With skin of yel - low hue.
3. Like theirs, but bright with heaven-ly grace, And filled with ho - ly light.

1. Some chil-dren see Him bronzed and brown, With dark and heav-y hair.
2. Some chil-dren see Him dark as they, And ah! they love Him, too!
3. Come wor-ship now the in - fant King, 'Tis love that's born to - night!

(Editor's note: verses may be re-ordered.)

William Hutson

Hymn
Alfred S. Burt

CHURCH YEAR — CHRISTMAS

31 Rise up, Shepherd, and Follow

1. There's a star in the each on___ Christ - mas morn,
2. If you take good heed to the an - gel's words,

Rise up shep-herd and fol - low,___ It will lead to the place where the
Rise up shep-herd and fol - low,___ You'll for - get your flocks, you'll for -

Christ was born,___ Rise up shep -herd and fol - low.___
get your herds,___ Rise up shep -herd and fol - low.___

Harmony

Fol - low, fol - low, Rise up shep-herd and fol - low,___

Traditional

Spiritual

CHURCH YEAR — CHRISTMAS

Fol-low the Star of Beth-le-hem, ___ Rise up shep-herd and fol-low. ___

32   Jesu, Jesu, Fill Us with Your Love

Refrain

Je - su, ___ Je - su, ___ Fill us with Your love, show

us how to serve the neigh-bors we have from You. ___

1. Kneels at the feet of His friends,   Si - lent - ly wash - es their
2. Neigh - bors are rich men and poor,   Neigh-bors are black men and
3. These are the ones we should serve,   These are the ones we should
4. Lov - ing puts us on our knees,   Serv - ing as though we are

1. feet,   Mas - ter who acts as a slave ___ to them.
2. white,   Neigh - bors are near - by and far ___ a - way.
3. love.   All men are neigh-bors to us ___ and You.
4. slaves,   This is the way we should live ___ with You.

Traditional, Ghana   Ghanaian Folk Song
Tr. Tom Colvin   *Collected and adapted, Tom Colvin*

CHURCH YEAR — PASSIONTIDE

33   Beneath the Cross of Jesus

1. Be - neath the cross of Je - sus I fain would take my stand,
2. Up - on the cross of Je - sus Mine eyes at times can see
3. I take, O cross, thy sha - dow For my a - bi - ding place;

1. The sha - dow of a might - y rock With - in a wea - ry land,
2. The ve - ry dy - ing form of one Who suf - fer'd there for me;
3. I ask no oth - er sun-shine than The sun - shine of His face;

1. A home with - in the wil - der - ness, A rest up - on the way,
2. And from my smit - ten heart with tears Two won - ders I con - fess:
3. Con - tent to let the world go by, To know no gain nor loss,

1. From the burn - ing of the noon-tide heat, And the bur - den of the day.
2. The won - ders of re - deem - ing love, And my own worth-less-ness.
3. My sin - ful self my on - ly shame, My glo - ry all the cross.

Elizabeth Clephane

Hymn
Frederick Maker

CHURCH YEAR — PASSIONTIDE

1. They crucified my Lord, _____ and He never said a mumbling word; They crucified my Lord, _____ and He never said a mumbling word. Not a word, not a word, _____ not a word.

2. They nailed Him to a tree, _____ and He never said a mumbling word; They nailed Him to a tree, _____ and He never said a mumbling word. Not a word, not a word, _____ not a word.

3. They pierced Him in the side, _____ and He never said a mumbling word; They pierced Him in the side, _____ and He never said a mumbling word. Not a word, not a word, _____ not a word.

Traditional   Spiritual

CHURCH YEAR — PASSIONTIDE

35   Jesus, Keep Me near the Cross

1. Je - sus, keep me   near the cross,   There   a pre - cious foun - tain
2. Near the cross, a   trem-bling soul,   Love   and mer - cy found me;
3. Near the cross! O   Lamb of God,   Bring its scenes be - fore   me;
4. Near the cross I'll   watch and wait,   Hop - ing, trust - ing ev - er,

1. Free   to all   a   heal - ing stream,   Flows from Cal - v'ry's moun - tain.
2. There the Bright and Morn - ing Star   Sheds its beams a - round   me.
3. Help me walk from day to day,   With its shad - ows o'er   me.
4. Till   I   reach the   gold - en strand,   Just be - yond the   riv - er.

Refrain

In   the cross,   in   the cross,   Be   my glo - ry   ev - er;

Till   my rap - tured soul shall find   Rest be - yond the   riv - er.

Fanny J. Crosby

Hymn
William H. Doane

CHURCH YEAR — PASSIONTIDE

36 Rock of Ages

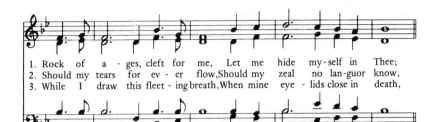

1. Rock of a - ges, cleft for me, Let me hide my-self in Thee;
2. Should my tears for ev - er flow, Should my zeal no lan-guor know,
3. While I draw this fleet - ing breath, When mine eye - lids close in death,

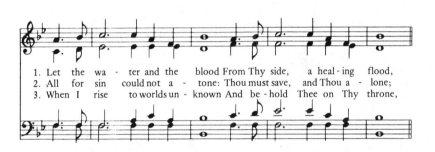

1. Let the wa - ter and the blood From Thy side, a heal - ing flood,
2. All for sin could not a - tone: Thou must save, and Thou a - lone;
3. When I rise to worlds un - known And be - hold Thee on Thy throne,

1. Be of sin the dou-ble cure, Cleanse me from its guilt and power.
2. In my hand no price I bring, Sim - ply to Thy cross I cling.
3. Rock of a - ges, cleft for me, Let me hide my-self in Thee. A - men.

Augustus M. Toplady

Hymn
Thomas Hastings

CHURCH YEAR — PASSIONTIDE

37 The Old Rugged Cross

1. On a hill far a - way stood an old rug - ged cross,
2. Oh, that old rug - ged cross so de - spised by the world,
3. In the old rug - ged cross, stained with blood so di - vine,
4. To the old rug - ged cross I will ev - er be true,

1. The em - blem of suf - fering and shame;
2. Has a won - drous at - trac - tion for me;
3. A won - drous beau - ty I see;
4. Its shame and re - proach glad - ly bear;

1. And I love that old cross where the dear - est and best
2. For the dear Lamb of God left His glo - ry a - bove,
3. For 'twas on that old cross Je - sus suf - fered and died,
4. Then He'll call me some day to my home far a - way,

1. For a world of lost sin - ners was slain.
2. To bear it to dark Cal - va - ry.
3. To par - don and sanc - ti - fy me.
4. Where His glo - ry for - ev - er I'll share.

George Bennard

Hymn
George Bennard

CHURCH YEAR — PASSIONTIDE

So I'll cher - ish the old rug - ged cross
cross, the old rug - ged cross,

Till my tro - phies at last I lay down;

I will cling to the old rug - ged cross,
cross, the old rug - ged cross,

And ex - change it some day for a crown.

38 Were You There

1. Were you there when they cru - ci - fied my Lord? Were you there? Were you there when they cru - ci - fied my Lord? Were you there? Oh, _____ some - times it caus - es me to trem - ble, trem - ble, trem - ble, _____ Were you

2. Were you there when they pierced Him in the side? Were you there? Were you there when they pierced Him in the side? Were you there? Oh, _____ some - times it caus - es me to trem - ble, trem - ble, trem - ble, _____ Were you

3. Were you there when they laid Him in the tomb? Were you there? Were you there when they laid Him in the tomb? Were you there? Oh, _____ some - times it caus - es me to trem - ble, trem - ble, trem - ble, _____ Were you

Traditional

Spiritual

CHURCH YEAR — PASSIONTIDE

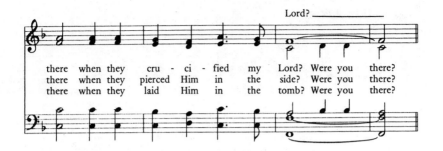

there when they cru - ci - fied my Lord? Were you there?
there when they pierced Him in the side? Were you there?
there when they laid Him in the tomb? Were you there?

39   When I Survey the Wondrous Cross

1. When I sur - vey the won - drous cross, On which the
2. For - bid it, Lord, that I should boast, Save in the
3. See, from His head, His hands, His feet, Sor - row and
4. Were the whole realm of na - ture mine, That were a

1. Prince of glo - ry died, My rich - est gain I
2. death of Christ, my God; All the vain things that
3. love flow min - gled down; Did e'er such love and
4. pres - ent far too small; Love so a - maz - ing,

1. count but loss, And pour con - tempt on all my pride.
2. charm me most, I sac - ri - fice them to His blood.
3. sor - row meet, Or thorns com - pose so rich a crown?
4. so di - vine, De - mands my soul, my life, my all.

Isaac Watts

Hymn
Gregorian Chant
Arr. Lowell Mason

40   He Arose

1. They   cru - ci - fied   my   Sav - ior   and   nailed Him   to   the
2.   Jo - seph begged   His   bod - y   and   laid   it   in   the
3.   Ma - ry,   she   came   run - ning,   a - look - ing   for   my
4. An   an - gel   came   from   heav - en   and   rolled the   stone   a -

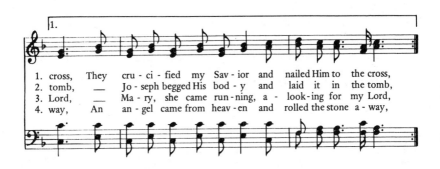

1. cross,   They   cru - ci - fied   my   Sav - ior   and   nailed Him to   the cross,
2. tomb, —   Jo - seph begged His   bod - y   and   laid   it   in   the tomb,
3. Lord, —   Ma - ry,   she   came   run - ning,   a - look - ing for   my Lord,
4. way,   An   an - gel   came   from   heav - en   and   rolled the stone a - way,

1. cross, — And the   Lord   shall bear   my   spir - it   home.
2. tomb, — And the   Lord   will   bear   my   spir - it   home.
3. Lord, — And the   Lord   will   bear   my   spir - it   home.
4. way, — And the   Lord   will   bear   my   spir - it   home.

Traditional

Spiritual
Willa A. Townsend

CHURCH YEAR — EASTER

CHURCH YEAR — EASTER

41   Am I a Soldier of the Cross

1. Am I a sol - dier of the cross, A
2. Must I be car - ried to the skies On
3. Are there no foes for me to face? Must
4. Sure I must fight, if I would reign: In -
5. Thy saints in all this glo - rious war Shall
6. When that il - lus - trious day shall rise, And

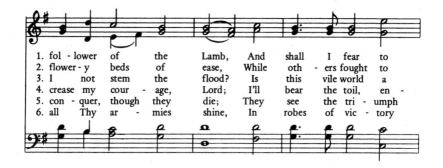

1. fol - lower of the Lamb, And shall I fear to
2. flower - y beds of ease, While oth - ers fought to
3. I not stem the flood? Is this vile world a
4. crease my cour - age, Lord; I'll bear the toil, en -
5. con - quer, though they die; They see the tri - umph
6. all Thy ar - mies shine, In robes of vic - tory

1. own His cause, Or blush to speak His name?
2. win the prize, And sailed through blood - y seas?
3. friend to grace, To help me on to God?
4. dure the pain, Sup - port - ed by Thy word.
5. from a - far, By faith they bring it nigh.
6. through the skies, The glo - ry shall be Thine.

Isaac Watts

Hymn
Thomas Arne

COMMITMENT

42　Done Made My Vow

Harmony

Done made my vow to the Lord, And I nev - er will turn back, Oh I will go, ___ I shall go to see what the end will be.

Unison　　　　　　　　　　　　*Harmony*

1. Some - times I'm up, some - times I'm down; See what the end will be, But
2. When I was a mourn-er just like you; See what the end will be, I

Unison　　　　　　　　　　　　*Harmony*

still my soul is heav'n-ly bound, See what the end will be.
prayed and prayed 'til I came through, See what the end will be.

Repeat Refrain after each stanza

Traditional

Spiritual
Arr. Evelyn Davidson White

Used by permission.

COMMITMENT

43   Down by the Riverside

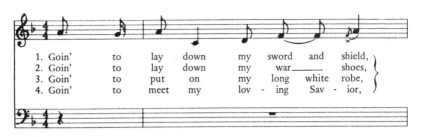

1. Goin'   to   lay   down   my   sword   and   shield,
2. Goin'   to   lay   down   my   war____   shoes,
3. Goin'   to   put   on   my   long   white   robe,
4. Goin'   to   meet   my   lov - ing   Sav - ior,

Refrain

Down   by   the   riv - er - side,   Down   by   the   riv - er - side,

Down   by   the   riv - er - side.

1. Goin'   to   lay down   my sword and shield,
2. Goin'   to   lay down   my war __   shoes,
3. Goin'   to   put on   my long white robe,
4. Goin'   to   meet my   lov - ing Sav - ior,

Down   by   the   riv - er - side,   To   stu - ud - y*   war __   no

* Like - "Stud-ee"

Traditional

Spiritual
Arr. Clarence W. White

COMMITMENT

COMMITMENT

44 Every Time I Feel the Spirit

Ev - 'ry - time I ___ feel the spir - it, ___ mov - ing

in my heart, __ I will pray. ___ Ev - 'ry - time I ___ feel the

spir - it, ___ mov - ing in my heart, ___ I will pray.

1. Up - on the moun - tain my Lord spoke, (Out of) His
2. ___ All a - round me looked so shine, Asked
3. ___ Jor - dan riv - er, chilly and cold, Chills the

Traditional   Spiritual

COMMITMENT

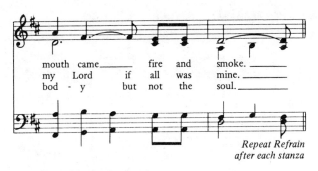

mouth came____ fire and smoke. ____
my Lord if all was mine. ____
bod - y but not the soul. ____

*Repeat Refrain
after each stanza*

45   O Holy Savior

1. O ho - ly Sav - ior! Friend un - seen, Since on Thine arm Thou bid'st me lean, Help me, thru - out life's chang - ing scene, By faith to cling to Thee!

2. What though the world deceitful prove,
   And earthly friends and joys remove?
   With patient, uncomplaining love
   Still I would cling to Thee.

3. Though faith and hope awhile be tried,
   I ask not, need not aught beside:
   How safe, how calm, how satisfied,
   The souls that cling to Thee.

Charlotte Elliott

Hymn
Ulysses Elam
Arr. R. Nathaniel Dett

COMMITMENT

46   I've Decided to Make Jesus My Choice

1. Some folk would rath - er have
2. These clothes may be rag - ged that I'm

1. hous - es and land. Some folk choose
2. wear - ing. Heav - y is the

Harrison Johnson

Gospel
Harrison Johnson
Arr. Kenneth Woods, Jr.

COMMITMENT

1. sil - ver and gold.
2. load that I'm bear - ing;

1. These things they treas - ure and for-
2. these old bur - dens that I'm

1. get a - bout their souls; I've de - cid - ed to make
2. car - rying

COMMITMENT

Je - sus my choice.

Refrain

The road is rough; the go - ing gets tough, and the

hills are hard to climb. I've start - ed out a

COMMITMENT

long time a - go; there's no doubt in my mind; I've de - cid - ed to make Je - sus my choice.

COMMITMENT

47   Just As I Am

1. Just as I am, with-out one plea, But that Thy
2. Just as I am, though tossed a-bout With ma-ny a
3. Just as I am, poor, wretch-ed, blind; Sight, rich-es,
4. Just as I am: Thou wilt re-ceive; Wilt wel-come,
5. Just as I am, Thy love un-known Has bro-ken
6. Just as I am, of Thy great love The breadth, length,

1. blood was shed for me, And that Thou bidd'st me
2. con-flict, ma-ny a doubt; Fight-ings and fears with-
3. heal-ing of the mind, Yea, all I need in
4. par-don, cleanse, re-lieve, Be-cause Thy prom-ise
5. ev-ery bar-rier down; Now to be Thine, yea,
6. depth, and height to prove, Here for a sea-son,

1. come to Thee, O Lamb of God, I come, I come.
2. in, with-out, O Lamb of God, I come, I come.
3. Thee to find, O Lamb of God, I come, I come.
4. I be-lieve, O Lamb of God, I come, I come.
5. Thine a-lone, O Lamb of God, I come, I come.
6. then a-bove: O Lamb of God, I come, I come. A-men.

Charlotte Elliott

Hymn
William B. Bradbury

COMMITMENT

48 My Faith Looks up to Thee

1. My faith looks up to Thee, Thou Lamb of
2. May Thy rich grace im - part Strength to my
3. While life's dark maze I tread, And griefs a -
4. When ends life's tran - sient dream, When death's cold,

1. Cal - va - ry, Sav - ior di - vine!
2. faint - ing heart, My zeal in - spire;
3. round me spread, Be Thou my guide;
4. sul - len stream Shall o'er me roll;

1. Now hear me while I pray, Take all my guilt a - way;
2. As Thou hast died for me, O may my love to Thee
3. Bid dark - ness turn to day, Wipe sor - row's tears a - way;
4. Blest Sav - ior, then in love, Fear and dis - trust re - move;

1. O let me from this day Be whol - ly Thine.
2. Pure, warm, and change - less be A liv - ing fire.
3. Nor let me ev - er stray From Thee a - side.
4. O bear me safe a - bove, A ran - somed soul. A - men.

Ray Palmer

Hymn
Lowell Mason

COMMITMENT

49   Softly and Tenderly Jesus Is Calling

1. Soft - ly and ten - der - ly Je - sus is call - ing,
2. Why should we tar - ry when Je - sus is plead - ing,
3. Time is now fleet - ing, the mo - ments are pass - ing,
4. Oh! for the won - der - ful love He has prom - ised,

1. Call - ing for you and for me; See, on the por - tals He's
2. Plead - ing for you and for me? Why should we lin - ger and
3. Pass - ing for you and for me; Shad - ows are gath - er - ing,
4. Prom - ised for you and for me; Tho' we have sinned, He has

1. wait - ing and watch - ing, Watch - ing for you and for me.
2. heed not His mer - cies, Mer - cies for you and for me?
3. death beds are com - ing, Com - ing for you and for me.
4. mer - cy and par - don, Par - don for you and for me.

William L. Thompson

Hymn
William L. Thompson

COMMITMENT

Refrain

Come home, come home,
Come home, come home,
Ye who are wea-ry, come home! Ear-nest-ly, ten-der-ly,
Je-sus is call-ing, Call-ing, O sin-ner, come home!

COMMITMENT

50   Yield Not to Temptation

1. Yield not to temp - ta - tion, For yield-ing is sin;
2. Shun e-vil com - pan - ion, Bad lan-guage dis - dain;
3. To him that o'er - com - eth, God giv - eth a crown;

1. Each vic - t'ry will help you Some oth - er to win;
2. God's name hold in rev - 'rence, Nor take it in vain;
3. Thro' faith we will con - quer, Tho' of-ten cast down;

1. Fight man - ful - ly on - ward, Dark pas-sions sub - due;
2. Be thought-ful and earn - est Kind - heart - ed and true;
3. He who is our Sav - ior, Our strength will re - new;

1. Look ev - er to Je - sus He'll car - ry you through.
2. Look ev - er to Je - sus He'll car - ry you through.
3. Look ev - er to Je - sus He'll car - ry you through.

Horatio R. Palmer

Hymn
Horatio R. Palmer

COMMITMENT

Refrain

Ask the Sav-ior to help you, Com-fort, strengthen, and keep you; He is will-ing to aid you, He will car-ry you through.

COMMITMENT

51   Free at Last

Free at last, free at last, I thank God I'm

free at last; Free at last, free at last, ____

I thank God I'm free at last. O free at last.

1. 'Way__ down yon-der in the grave - yard walk, I thank God I'm
2. On a my knees when the light pass'd by, I thank God I'm
3. Some of these morn - ings,__ bright and fair, I thank God I'm

Traditional

Spiritual
Arr. John W. Work

COMMUNITY

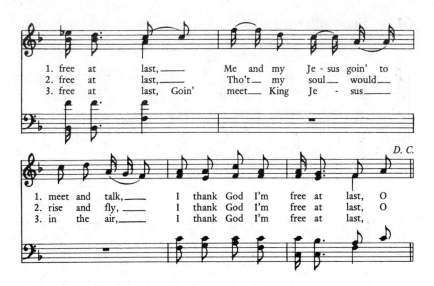

1. free at last,____ Me and my Je - sus goin' to
2. free at last,____ Tho't__ my soul__ would__
3. free at last, Goin' meet__ King Je - sus____

D. C.

1. meet and talk,____ I thank God I'm free at last, O
2. rise and fly,____ I thank God I'm free at last, O
3. in the air,____ I thank God I'm free at last,

52   I Love Thy Kingdom, Lord

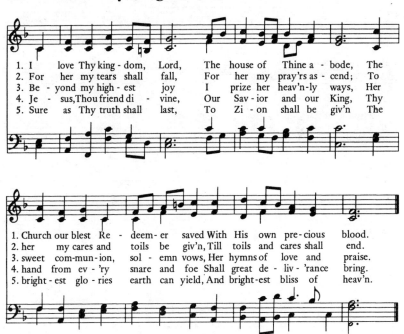

1. I love Thy king - dom, Lord, The house of Thine a - bode, The
2. For her my tears shall fall, For her my pray'rs as - cend; To
3. Be - yond my high - est joy I prize her heav'n - ly ways, Her
4. Je - sus, Thou friend di - vine, Our Sav - ior and our King, Thy
5. Sure as Thy truth shall last, To Zi - on shall be giv'n The

1. Church our blest Re - deem - er saved With His own pre - cious blood.
2. her my cares and toils be giv'n, Till toils and cares shall end.
3. sweet com - mun - ion, sol - emn vows, Her hymns of love and praise.
4. hand from ev - 'ry snare and foe Shall great de - liv - 'rance bring.
5. bright - est glo - ries earth can yield, And bright - est bliss of heav'n.

Timothy Dwight

Hymn
Aaron Williams

COMMUNITY

53 God of Our Fathers

1. God of our fa - thers, whose al - might - y hand
2. Thy love di - vine hath led us in the past,
3. From war's a - larms, from dead - ly pes - ti - lence,
4. Re - fresh thy peo - ple on their toil - some way,

1. Leads forth in beau - ty all the star - ry band
2. In this free land by thee our lot is cast;
3. Be thy strong arm our ev - er sure de - fence;
4. Lead us from night to nev - er - end - ing day;

1. Of shin - ing worlds in splen - dor through the skies,
2. Be thou our rul - er, guard - ian, guide, and stay,
3. Thy true re - li - gion in our hearts in - crease,
4. Fill all our lives with love and grace di - vine,

1. Our grate - ful songs be - fore thy throne a - rise.
2. Thy word our law, thy paths our cho - sen way.
3. Thy boun - teous good - ness nour - ish us in peace.
4. And glo - ry, laud, and praise be ev - er thine.

Daniel C. Roberts

Hymn
George W. Warner

COMMUNITY

54 I Couldn't Hear Nobody Pray

1. I could-n't hear no-bod-y pray, I could-n't hear no-bod-y pray. I was way down yon-der by my-self, And I could-n't hear no-bod-y pray, my Lord.

2. So burden I couldn't hear nobody pray,
   Ain't it sad I couldn't hear nobody pray?
   Refrain

3. Ain't it lonesome, I couldn't hear nobody pray?
   Come to Jesus, I couldn't hear nobody pray.
   Refrain

Traditional

Spiritual
Arr. Harry T. Burleigh

COMMUNITY

55   I'm A'Going to Eat at the Welcome Table

1. I'm ____ a-going to eat at the wel-come ta - ble,
2. I'm ____ a-going to feast on milk __ and hon - ey,
3. I'm ____ a-going to fly all a-round in Heav - en,
4. I'm ____ a-going to wade cross Jor - dan's riv - er,

1. I'm ____ a-going to eat at the wel-come ta - ble, some of these days. __
2. I'm ____ a-going to feast on __ milk and hon-ey, some of these days. __
3. I'm ____ a-going to fly all a-round in Heav-en, some of these days. __
4. I'm ____ a-going to wade cross __ Jor-dan's riv - er, some of these days. __

1. I'm ____ a-going to eat at the wel - come ta - - ble, I'm going to
2. I'm ____ a-going to feast on milk __ and hon - ey, I'm going to
3. I'm ____ a-going to fly all a-round in Heav - en, I'm going to
4. I'm ____ a-going to wade cross Jor - dan's riv - er, I'm going to

1. eat at the wel - come ta - ble, some of these days.
2. feast on __ milk and hon - ey, some of these days.
3. fly all a-round in Heav - en, some of these days.
4. wade 'cross __ Jor - dan's riv - er, some of these days.

Traditional

Spiritual
Arr. Carl Diton

COMMUNITY

56 Jesus, We Want to Meet

1. Je - sus, we want__ to meet On this __ thy
2. We kneel in awe __ and fear On this __ thy
3. Thy bless - ing, Lord,__ we seek On this __ thy
4. Our minds we ded - i - cate On this__ thy

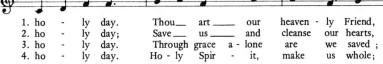

1. ho - ly day; We gath - er round_ thy throne On this__ thy
2. ho - ly day; ; Pray God to teach__ us here On this__ thy
3. ho - ly day; Give joy of thy vic-to - ry On this__ thy
4. ho - ly day; Heart and soul con - se - crate On this__ thy

1. ho - ly day. Thou__ art ____ our heaven - ly Friend,
2. ho - ly day; Save __ us ____ and cleanse our hearts,
3. ho - ly day. Through grace a - lone are we saved ;
4. ho - ly day. Ho - ly Spir - it, make us whole;

1. Hear our prayers as they as - cend; Look in - to our hearts and
2. Lead and guide our acts of praise, And our faith from seed to
3. In thy flock may we be found; Let the mind of Christ a -
4. Bless the ser - mon in this place; And __ as we go, __

1. minds to - day, On this ___ thy ho - ly day.
2. flow - er raise, On this ___ thy ho - ly day.
3. bide in us On this ___ thy ho - ly day.
4. lead us Lord; We shall be thine ev - er - more.

A. T. Olajide Olude
Tr. Biodum Adebesin
Versed, Austin C. Lovelace

Nigerian Folk Song
Transcribed and arranged,
A. T. Olajide

COMMUNITY

57 Lord, Dismiss Us with Thy Blessing

1. Lord, dis - miss us with Thy bless - ing; Fill our hearts with
2. Thanks we give and ad - o - ra - tion For Thy Gos - pel's
3. So that when Thy love shall call us, Sav - ior, from the

1. joy and peace; Let us each, Thy love pos - sess - ing,
2. joy - ful sound: May the fruits of Thy sal - va - tion
3. world a - way, Fear of death shall not ap - pall us,

1. Tri - umph in re - deem - ing grace: O re - fresh us,
2. In our hearts and lives a - bound: May Thy pres - ence,
3. Glad Thy sum - mons to o - bey. May we ev - er,

1. O re - fresh us, Trav -'ling thro' this wil - der - ness.
2. may Thy pres-ence With us ev - er - more be found;
3. may we ev - er Reign with Thee in end - less day. A - men.

Attributed to John Fawcett

Hymn
Sicilian Melody

COMMUNITY

58 Reach out and Touch Somebody's Hand

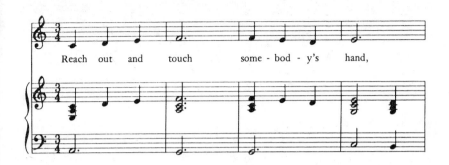

Reach out and touch some - bod - y's hand,

Make this world a bet - ter place _____ if you can;

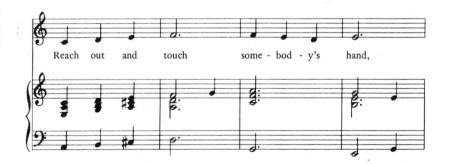

Reach out and touch some - bod - y's hand,

Nick Ashford and Valerie Simpson

Gospel
Nick Ashford and Valerie Simpson
Arr. Richard Smallwood

COMMUNITY

Make this world a bet-ter place _____ if you can. can.

1. (Just try) Take a lit - tle time out of your bus - y day to
2. (Just try) If you see an old friend on the street and he's

1. give en - cour-age - ment to some - one who's lost the way; _
2. down re - mem - ber his shoes could fit your_ feet; _

COMMUNITY

D. C.

1. (Just try) or would I be talk - ing to a stone. If
2. (Just try) a lit - tle kind - ness and you'll see. It's

1. I asked you to share a prob - lem that's not your own, _____
2. something that comes ver - y nat - u - ral - ly. _____

___ We can change things if we start giv - ing. Why don't you

COMMUNITY

59   Savior, Like a Shepherd Lead Us

1. Sav - ior, like a shep - herd lead us,
2. We are Thine; do Thou be - friend us,
3. Thou hast prom - ised to re - ceive us,
4. Ear - ly let us seek Thy fa - vor;

1. Much we need Thy ten - der care; In Thy pleas-ant pas-tures
2. Be the Guard-ian of our way; Keep Thy flock, from sin de -
3. Poor and sin - ful tho' we be; Thou hast mer - cy to re -
4. Ear - ly let us do Thy will; Bless - ed Lord and on - ly

1. feed us, For our use Thy folds pre - pare.
2. fend us, Seek us when we go a - stray.
3. lieve us, Grace to cleanse, and power to free.
4. Sav - ior, With Thy love our bos - oms fill.

Dorothy A. Thrupp

Hymn
William B. Bradbury

COMMUNITY

1. Bless - ed Je - sus, Bless - ed Je - sus, Thou hast
2. Bless - ed Je - sus, Bless - ed Je - sus, Hear Thy
3. Bless - ed Je - sus, Bless - ed Je - sus, Ear - ly
4. Bless - ed Je - sus, Bless - ed Je - sus, Thou hast

1. bought us, Thine we are; Bless - ed Je - sus, Bless - ed
2. chil - dren when they pray; Bless - ed Je - sus, Bless - ed
3. let us turn to Thee; Bless - ed Je - sus, Bless - ed
4. lov'd us, love us still; Bless - ed Je - sus, Bless - ed

1. Je - sus, Thou hast bought us, Thine we are.
2. Je - sus, Hear Thy chil - dren when they pray.
3. Je - sus, Ear - ly let us turn to Thee.
4. Je - sus, Thou hast lov'd us, love us still. A - men.

COMMUNITY

60 Shall We Gather at the River

1. Shall we gath-er at the riv - er, Where bright an-gel feet have trod;
2. On the mar-gin of the riv - er, Wash-ing up its sil - ver spray,
3. Ere we reach the shin-ing riv - er, Lay we ev-'ry bur-den down;
4. Soon we'll reach the shin-ing riv - er, Soon our pil-grim-age will cease,

1. With its crys - tal tide for - ev - er Flow-ing by the throne of God?
2. We will walk and wor-ship ev - er, All the hap-py gold - en day.
3. Grace our spir - its will de - liv - er, And pro-vide a robe and crown.
4. Soon our hap - py hearts will quiv - er With the mel - o - dy of peace.

Refrain

Yes, we'll gath-er at the riv - er, The beau-ti-ful, the beau-ti-ful riv - er;

Gath-er with the saints at the riv - er That flows by the throne of God.

Robert Lowry

Hymn
Robert Lowry

COMMUNITY

61   Steal Away

Steal a-way, steal a-way, steal a-way to Je - sus!

Steal a-way, steal a-way home, I ain't got long to stay here!

1. My Lord ___ calls me, He calls me by the thun - der;
2. Green trees are bend - ing, Poor sin - ner stands a - trem - bling;
3. Tomb stones are burst - ing, Poor sin - ner stands a - trem - bling;
4. My Lord ___ calls me, He calls me by the light - ning,

The trum-pet sounds with - in - a my soul, I ain't got long to stay here.

Traditional

Spiritual
Arr. Edward C. Deas

COMMUNITY

62   Sweet, Sweet Spirit

1. There's a sweet, sweet Spir-it in this place, _____ and I
(2. There are) bless-ings you can-not re - ceive _____ till you
(3. If you) say He saved you from your sin, _____ now you're

1. know that it's the Spir - it of __the Lord. _____ There are
2. know Him in His full - ness, and __ be - lieve. _____ You're the
3. weak, you're bound, and can - not en - ter in, _____ you can

Doris Akers

Gospel
Doris Akers

COMMUNITY

1. sweet ex - press-ions on each face, _____ and I
2. one to pro-fit when you say, _____ "I am
3. make it right if you will yield; _____ you'll en -

1. know they feel the pres - ence of __ the Lord. _____
2. going to walk with Je - sus all __ the way." _____
3. joy the Ho - ly Spir - it that __ we feel. _____

Sweet Ho - ly Spir - it, Sweet Heav-en-ly Dove,

COMMUNITY

stay right here with us,＿ fill- ing us with＿your love.

And for these bless - ings ＿＿＿ we lift our hearts in

praise; with-out a doubt we'll know＿ that we have

1. –2.　　**3.**

been re - vived＿when we shall leave this place. 2.There are
　　　　　　　　　　　　　　　　　3. if you place.

rit.

COMMUNITY

63 We Gather Together

1. We gath - er to - geth - er to ask the Lord's bless - ing;
2. Be - side us to guide us, our God with us join - ing,
3. We all do ex - tol thee, thou lead - er tri - umph - ant,

1. He chast - ens and hast - ens his will to make known;
2. Or - dain - ing, main - tain - ing his king - dom di - vine;
3. And pray that thou still our de - fend - er wilt be.

1. The wick - ed op - press - ing now cease from dis - tress - ing:
2. So from the be - gin - ning the fight we were win - ning:
3. Let thy con - gre - ga - tion es - cape trib - u - la - tion:

1. Sing prais - es to his Name; he for - gets not his own.
2. Thou, Lord, wast at our side: all glo - ry be thine!
3. Thy Name be ev - er praised! O Lord, make us free! A - men.

Anonymous

Hymn
Traditional Netherlands Melody
Arr. Edward Kremser

COMMUNITY

64   We've Come This Far by Faith

We've come this far___ by___ faith,   Lean - ing on the

Lord; ___   Trust - ing in his ho - ly   word,

He's nev-er failed___ me   yet.   O _____

Albert A. Goodson

Gospel
Albert A. Goodson
Arr. Richard Smallwood

COMMUNITY

can't turn a - round, _____ We've come this far by faith. _____

Don't be dis-cour-aged _ when trou-ble's _ in your life, He'll bear your

bur - dens and move all mis - er - y and strife. That's why we've

2. Just the other day I heard a man say
   He didn't believe in God's word;
   But I can truly say that God has made a way and He's never failed me yet.
   That's why we've

   Refrain

COMMUNITY

65 What a Fellowship

1. What a fel - low-ship, what a joy di - vine,
2. Oh, how sweet to walk in the pil - grim way,
3. What have I to dread, what have I to fear,

Lean - ing on the ev - er - last - ing arms; What a bless - ed-ness,
Lean - ing on the ev - er - last - ing arms; Oh, how bright the path
Lean - ing on the ev - er - last - ing arms; I have bless - ed peace

what a peace is mine, Lean - ing on the ev - er - last - ing arms.
grows from day to day, Lean - ing on the ev - er - last - ing arms.
with my Lord so near, Lean - ing on the ev - er - last - ing arms.

Refrain

Lean - ing, lean - ing,
Lean - ing on Je - sus, Lean - ing on Je - sus,

A. E. Hoffman

Hymn
A. J. Showalter

COMMUNITY

Safe and se-cure from all a-larms; Lean - ing,
Lean - ing on Je - sus,

lean - ing, Lean - ing on the ev-er - last-ing arms.
Lean - ing on Je - sus,

66　Thank You, Lord

1. Thank you Lord, Thank you Lord, Thank you
2. Been so good, Been so good, Been so
3. Been my friend, Been my friend, Been my

1. Lord,——
2. good,—— I just want to thank you Lord.
3. friend,——

Contemporary

Gospel
Arr. Richard Smallwood

COMMUNITY

67 Nobody Knows the Trouble I've Seen

Unison

No - bod - y knows the trou - ble I've seen,

No - bod - y knows but Je - sus, No - bod - y knows the

trou - ble I've seen, Glo - ry, hal - le - lu - jah.

1. Some - times I'm up, some - times I'm down, Oh, yes, Lord, Some -
2. Al - though you see me going 'long so, Oh, yes, Lord, I

times I'm al - most to the ground,__ Oh, yes, Lord.
have my trou - bles here be - low, __ Oh, yes, Lord.

*D. C. after
each stanza*

Traditional

Spiritual

FAITH

68 There's a Wideness in God's Mercy

1. There's a wide-ness in God's mer-cy Like the wide-ness of the sea;
2. There is no place where earth's sor-rows Are more felt than up in heav'n;
3. For the love of God is broad-er Than the meas-ure of man's mind;

There's a kind-ness in his jus-tice, Which is more than lib-er-ty.
There is no place where earth's fail-ings Have such kind-ly judg-ment giv'n.
And the heart of the E-ter-nal Is most won-der-ful-ly kind.

There is wel-come for the sin-ner, And more gra-ces for the good;
There is plen-ti-ful re-demp-tion In the blood that has been shed;
If our love were but more sim-ple, We should take him at his word;

There is mer-cy with the Sav-iour; There is heal-ing in his blood.
There is joy for all the mem-bers In the sor-rows of the Head.
And our lives would be all sun-shine In the sweet-ness of the Lord.

Frederick William Faber

Hymn
John Zundel

FAITH

69 Do Lord Remember Me

1. Do Lord, ___ do Lord, Do re-mem-ber me,
2. When I'm in trou-ble, Do re-mem-ber me,
3. When I'm ___ dy-in', Do re-mem-ber me,
4. When this world's on fire, Do re-mem-ber me,

1. Do Lord, ___ do Lord, Do re-mem-ber me, ___
2. When I'm in trou-ble, Do re-mem-ber me, ___
3. When I'm ___ dy-in', Do re-mem-ber me, ___
4. When this world's on fire, Do re-mem-ber me, ___

1. Do Lord, ___ do Lord, Do re-mem-ber me,
2. When I'm in trou-ble, Do re-mem-ber me,
3. When I'm ___ dy-in', Do re-mem-ber me,
4. When this world's on fire, Do re-mem-ber me,

O

Do Lord re-mem-ber me.

Traditional

Spiritual
Arr. John W. Work

MISSION

70   Here Am I, Send Me

1. Hark! the voice of Je - sus call - ing, Who will
2. Let none hear you i - dly say - ing, There is
3. Take the task He gives you glad - ly, Let His

1. go and work to - day? Fields are white, the har - vest
2. noth - ing I can do; While the souls of men are
3. work your pleas - ure be; An - swer quick - ly when He

1. wait - ing, Who will bear the sheaves a - way?
2. dy - ing, And the Mas - ter calls for you.
3. call - eth, "Here am I, send me, send me."

Refrain

Loud and long the Mas-ter call-eth, Rich re - ward He of - fers free;

Who will an - swer, glad-ly say-ing, "Here am I, send me, send me."

Daniel March

Hymn
J. C. Lenderman

MISSION

71   Bless the Lord

Bless the Lord, O my soul,__ and all that is with-
in me, Bless His Ho - ly Name.__
He has done great things, He has done great things,__
He has done great things, Bless His Ho - ly Name.__

Contemporary

Gospel
Andrae Crouch
Arr. Richard Smallwood

PRAISE

72 Come Sunday

(Refrain) Oo _____ Oo _____

Sun-day, oh come Sun-day, That's the day. _____

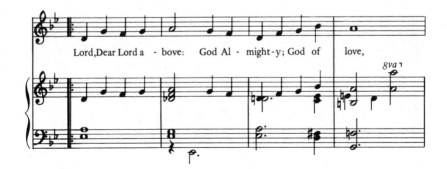

Lord, Dear Lord a - bove: God Al - might-y; God of love,

Duke Ellington

Selection, Suite "Black, Brown and Beige"
Duke Ellington

PRAISE

Please look down and see my peo - ple through. _____

1. I be - lieve that God put sun and moon up in the
2. Heav - en is a good - ness time. A bright - er light on
3. I be - lieve God is now, was then and al - ways will

1. sky. I don't mind the gray skies, 'cause they're
2. high. Do unto others as you would have them do to you, and
3. be. With God's bless - ing we can make it

1. just clouds pass - ing by.
2. have a bright - er by and by. Lord, Dear Lord a -
3. through e - ter - ni - ty.

bove: God Al - might - y; God of love,

1. 2.

Please look down and see my peo - ple through. _____

PRAISE

73   Didn't My Lord Deliver Daniel?

Did - n't my Lord__ de - liv - er Dan - iel,___ De - liv - er

Dan - iel,__ de-liv-er Dan - iel,__ Did-n't my Lord__ de - liv - er

Dan - iel,__ And why not_____ ev - er - y man.

1. He de - liv - er'd Dan - iel from the li - on's den, ____
2. The wind blows east and the wind blows west, It

Traditional   Spiritual

PRAISE

Jo - nah from the bel - ly of the whale, And the
blows like the judge - ment day, And

He - brew chil - dren from the fie - ry __ fur - nace, And
ev - 'ry soul __ that __ nev - er did pray __ will be

why not __ ev - er - y __ man.
glad __ to pray __ that __ day.

Repeat Refrain
after each stanza

74 Down at the Cross

1. Down at the cross where my Sav - ior died,
2. I am so won - drous - ly saved from sin,
3. O, pre - cious foun - tain that saves from sin,
4. Come to this foun - tain so rich and sweet;

1. Down where for cleans-ing from sin I cried, There to my heart was the
2. Je - sus so sweet-ly a - bides with-in, There at the cross where He
3. I am so glad I have en - tered in; There Je-sus saves me and
4. Cast your poor soul at the Sav-ior's feet; Plunge in to-day, and be

1. blood ap - plied;
2. took me in;
3. keeps me clean;   Glo - ry to His name.
4. made com - plete;

Glo - ry to His name, Glo - ry to His name,

Elisha A. Hoffman

Hymn
John H. Stockton

PRAISE

There to my heart was the blood ap-plied. Glo-ry to His name.

75 Come, Thou Almighty King

1. Come, Thou al-might-y King, Help us Thy Name to sing, Help us to praise. Fa-ther whose love un-known All things cre-a-ted own, Build in our hearts Thy throne, An-cient of Days.
2. Come, Thou In-car-nate Word, By heav'n and earth a-dored; Our pray'r at-tend: Come, and Thy peo-ple bless; Come, give Thy word suc-cess; Stab-lish Thy right-eous-ness, Sav-ior and friend.
3. Come, Ho-ly Com-fort-er, Thy sa-cred wit-ness bear In this glad hour: Thou, who al-might-y art, Now rule in ev-'ry heart, And ne'er from us de-part, Spir-it of pow'r.
4. To Thee, great One in Three, The high-est prais-es be, Hence ev-er more; Thy sov-'reign maj-es-ty May we in glo-ry see, And to e-ter-ni-ty Love and a-dore. A-men.

Anonymous

Hymn
Felice De Giardini

PRAISE

76 Come, Thou Fount of Every Blessing

1. Come, Thou Fount of ev-ery bless-ing, Tune my heart to sing Thy grace;
2. Here I raise my Eb-en - e - zer; Hith-er by Thy help I'm come;
3. O, to grace how great a debt - or Dai-ly I'm con-strained to be;

1. Streams of mer - cy nev-er ceas-ing, Call for songs of loud-est praise.
2. And I hope, by Thy good pleas-ure, Safe-ly to ar - rive at home.
3. Let that grace, Lord, like a fet - ter, Bind my wan-d'ring heart to Thee.

1. Teach me some me - lo-dious son - net, Sung by flam-ing tongues a - bove:
2. Je - sus sought me when a stran - ger, Wan-d'ring from the fold of God:
3. Prone to wan - der, Lord, I feel it; Prone to leave the God I love:

1. Praise the mount, O fix me on it. Mount of God's un-chang-ing love.
2. He, to save my soul from dan-ger, In - ter-posed His pre-cious blood.
3. Here's my heart, Lord, take and seal it; Seal it from Thy courts a - bove. A - men.

Robert Robinson

Hymn
J. Wyeth's Collection

PRAISE

77 Fairest Lord Jesus

1. Fair - est Lord Je - sus, Rul - er of all
2. Fair are the mea - dows, Fair - er still the
3. Fair is the sun - shine, Fair - er still the

1. na - ture, O Thou of God and man the Son;
2. wood-lands, Robed in the bloom-ing garb of spring:
3. moon-light, And all the twink - ling, star - ry host:

Org.

1. Thee will I cher - ish, Thee will I hon - or,
2. Je - sus is fair - er, Je - sus is pur - er,
3. Je - sus shines bright - er, Je - sus shines pur - er,

1. Thou, my soul's glo - ry, joy, and crown.
2. Who makes the woe - ful heart to sing.
3. Than all the an - gels heav'n can boast.

Anonymous

Hymn
Silesian Melody

PRAISE

78 Hallelujah

Extra Verses

2. Lord we praise thee, *(8 times)*
3. Lord we thank thee, *(8 times)*

Contemporary

Gospel
Arr. Richard Smallwood

PRAISE

79　He Is King of Kings

Traditional

Spiritual
Arr. Horace Clarence Boyer

PRAISE

80　Holy, Holy, Holy, Lord God Almighty

1. Ho - ly, Ho - ly, Ho - ly! Lord God Al - might - y!
2. Ho - ly, Ho - ly, Ho - ly! all the saints a - dore Thee,
3. Ho - ly, Ho - ly, Ho - ly! though the dark - ness hide Thee,
4. Ho - ly, Ho - ly, Ho - ly! Lord God Al - might - y!

1. Ear - ly in the morn - ing our song shall rise to Thee:
2. Cast - ing down their gold - en crowns a - round the glass - y sea;
3. Though the eye of sin - ful man Thy glo - ry may not see,
4. All Thy works shall praise Thy Name, in earth, and sky, and sea;

1. Ho - ly, Ho - ly, Ho - ly! mer - ci - ful and might - y,
2. Cher - u - bim and ser - a - phim fall - ing down be - fore Thee,
3. On - ly Thou art ho - ly; there is none be - side Thee,
4. Ho - ly, Ho - ly, Ho - ly! mer - ci - ful and might - y!

1. God in three Per - sons, bless - ed Trin - i - ty!
2. Which wert and art, and ev - er - more shalt be.
3. Per - fect in pow'r, in love, and pu - ri - ty.
4. God in three Per - sons, bless - ed Trin - i - ty! A - men.

Reginald Heber

Hymn
John B. Dykes

PRAISE

81   I Want to Be Ready

Refrain

I want to be read-y, I want to be read-y,

I want to be read-y To walk in Je-ru-sa-lem just like John.

1. John said that Je-ru-sa-lem was four-square,
2. When Pe-ter was preach-ing at Pen-te-cost,

1. I hope, good Lord, I'll
2. O he was filled with the

1. Walk in Je-ru-sa-lem just like John.
2. Walk in Je-ru-sa-lem just like John.

1. meet you there,
2. Ho-ly Ghost,

D. C.

1. Walk in Je-ru-sa-lem just like John.
2. Walk in Je-ru-sa-lem just like John.

Traditional

Spiritual
Arr. R. Nathaniel Dett

PRAISE

82   How Great Thou Art

With strength

1. O Lord my God, when I in awe-some
2. When thro' the woods and for-est glades I
3. And when I think that God, his Son not
4. When Christ shall come with shout of ac-cla-

won-der con-sid-er all the worlds* thy hands have
wan-der and hear the birds sing sweet-ly in the
spar-ing, sent him to die, I scarce can take it
ma-tion and take me home, what joy shall fill my

made,____ I see the stars, I hear the roll-ing*
trees,____ when I look down from loft-y moun-tain
in,____ that on the cross, my bur-den glad-ly
heart!____ Then I shall bow in hum-ble ad-o-

thun-der, thy pow'r thro'-out the u-ni-verse dis-played.__
gran-deur, and hear the brook and feel the gen-tle breeze.__
bear-ing, he bled and died to take a-way my sin.__
ra-tion, and there pro-claim, my God, how great thou art.__

* The translator's original words are "works" and "mighty."

Stuart K. Hine

Anthem
Swedish Folk Melody,
Arr. Stuart K. Hine

PRAISE

Then sings my soul, my Sav - ior, God, to Thee;___ How great Thou

art,___ how great Thou art!___ Then sings my soul, my Sav - ior God, to

Thee:___ How great Thou art,___ how great Thou art!___

83 Jesu, Joy of Man's Desiring

1. Je - su joy of man's de - sir - ing, Ho - ly
2. Thro' the way where hope is guid - ing, Hark what

1. wis - dom love most bright. Drawn by thee our souls as -
2. peace - ful mu - sic rings Where the flock in thee con -

1. pir - ing Soar to un - cre - a - ted light.
2. fid - ing Drink of joy from death - less springs.

1. Word of God, our flesh that fash-ioned with the fire of
2. Theirs is beau - ty's fair - est pleas-ure, theirs is wis - dom's

Martin Janus

Hymn
Johann Schop
Arr. and Har. J. S. Bach

PRAISE

1. life im - pas - sioned. Striv - ing still to truth un -
2. ho - liest treas - ures. Thou dost e - ven lead

1. known Soar - ing, dy - ing round thy throne.
2. thine own In the love of joys un - known.

84 King Jesus is A'Listenin'

Refrain

King Je - sus is a - lis - ten - in', All day long,_ King
Je - sus is a - lis - ten - in', All day long,_ King Je - sus is a -
lis - ten - in', All day long,_ to hear some sin - ner pray.

Fine

1. Some say that John the Bap - tist Was
2. That Gos - pel train is com - in', A -
3. I know I've been con - vert - ed, I

Traditional

Spiritual
Traditional

PRAISE

D. C.

1. noth - in'___ but___ a Jew, But the Ho - ly Bi - ble
2. rum - blin'___ thru___ the land, But I hear them wheels a -
3. ain't gon - na make no a - larm, For my soul is bound to

1. tells us That___ John___ was a preach - er, too.
2. hum - min', Get___ read - y to board___ that train!
3. Je - sus, And the dev - il can't___ do me no harm.

PRAISE

85 Love Divine, All Loves Excelling

1. Love di - vine, all loves ex - cell - ing, Joy of heav'n, to
2. Come, Al - might - y to de - liv - er, Let us all Thy
3. Fin - ish, then, Thy new cre - a - tion; Pure and spot - less

1. earth come down; Fix in us Thy hum - ble dwell - ing;
2. grace re - ceive; Sud - den - ly re - turn, and nev - er,
3. let us be; Let us see Thy great sal - va - tion

1. All Thy faith - ful mer - cies crown. Je - sus, Thou art all com - pas - sion.
2. Nev - er more Thy tem - ples leave. Thee we would be al - ways bless - ing,
3. Per - fect - ly re - stored in Thee: Changed from glo - ry in - to glo - ry,

1. Pure un - bound - ed love Thou art; Vis - it us with
2. Serve Thee as thy hosts a - bove, Pray, and praise Thee
3. Till in heav'n we take our place, Till we cast our

Charles Wesley

Hymn
John Zundel

PRAISE

1. Thy sal - va - tion; En - ter ev - 'ry trem - bling heart.
2. with - out ceas - ing, Glo - ry in Thy per - fect love.
3. crowns be - fore Thee, Lost in won - der, love, and praise. A - men.

86 From All That Dwell Below the Skies

1. From all that dwell be - low the skies Let the Cre - a - tor's
2. E - ter - nal are Thy mer - cies, Lord, And truth e - ter - nal
3. Praise God, from Whom all bless - ings flow; Praise Him, all crea - tures

1. praise a - rise! Let the Re - deem - er's Name be
2. is Thy word: Thy praise shall sound from shore to
3. here be - low; Praise Him a - bove, ye heav'n - ly

1. sung Thro' ev - 'ry land, by ev - 'ry tongue!
2. shore Till suns shall rise and set no more.
3. host: Praise Fa - ther, Son, and Ho - ly Ghost. A - men.

Isaac Watts
Doxology, Thomas Ken

Hymn
Louis Bourgeois

PRAISE

87   O How I Love Jesus

1. A - las, and did my Sav-iour bleed, And did my Sov - 'reign die?
2. Was it for crimes that I have done He groaned up-on the tree?
3. Well might the sun in dark-ness hide, And shut his glo - ries in,
4. Thus might I hide my blush-ing face While His dear cross ap - pears;
5. But drops of grief can ne'er re-pay The debt of love I owe;

1. Would He de - vote that sa-cred head For such a worm as I?
2. A - maz-ing pit - y! grace un - known! And love be-yond de - gree!
3. When Christ, the great Cre - a - tor, died For man, the crea-ture's sin.
4. Dis - solve, my heart in thank-ful - ness, And melt mine eyes to tears.
5. Here, Lord, I give my - self a - way, 'Tis all that I can do.

Refrain

O how I love Je - sus! O how I love Je - sus!
I'll nev - er for - get Him, I'll nev - er for - get Him,

O how I love Je - sus! Be - cause He first loved me.
I'll nev - er for - get Him, O Lord, re-mem - ber me!

Isaac Watts

Hymn
Arr. Edward C. Deas

PRAISE

88 Revive Us Again

1. We praise Thee, O God, For the Son of Thy
2. We praise Thee, O God, For Thy spir - it of
3. All glo - ry and praise To the Lamb that was
4. Re - vive us a - gain; Fill each heart with Thy

1. love, For Je - sus who died And is now gone a - bove.
2. light, Who has shown us our Sav - ior, And scat - tered our night.
3. slain, Who has borne all our sins And has cleansed ev - 'ry stain.
4. love, May each soul be re - kin - dled With fire from a - bove.

Refrain

Hal - le - lu - jah! Thine the glo - ry, Hal - le - lu - jah! A -

men; Hal - le - lu - jah! Thine the glo - ry, Re - vive us a - gain.

William P. MacKay

Hymn
John J. Husband

PRAISE

89 On Our Way Rejoicing

1. On our way re - joic - ing Glad - ly let us go;
2. If with hon - est - heart - ed Love for God and man,
3. Un - to God the Fa - ther Joy - ful songs we sing,

1. Con - quer'd hath our Lead - er, Van - quish'd is the foe.
2. Day by day Thou find us Do - ing what we can,
3. Un - to God the Sav - ior Thank - ful hearts we bring,

1. Christ with - out, our safe - ty; Christ with - in, our joy;
2. Thou who giv'st the seed - time Wilt give large in - crease,
3. Un - to God the Spir - it Bow we and a - dore,

1. Who, if we be faith - ful, Can our hope de - stroy?
2. Crown the head with bless - ings, Fill the heart with peace.
3. On our way re - joic - ing Now and ev - er - more.

John S. B. Monsell

Hymn
Frances R. Havergal

PRAISE

Refrain

On our way re - joic - ing As we for - ward move,

Heark - en to our prais - es, O Thou God of love! A - men.

90   Take Your Burden to the Lord (Leave It There)

1. If the world from you with-hold of its
2. If your bod - y suf - fers pain and your
3. When your en - e - mies as - sail and your
4. When your youth - ful days are gone and old

1. sil - ver and its gold, And you have to get a - long with mea - ger
2. health you can't re-gain, And your soul is al - most sink - ing in de-
3. heart be-gins to fail, Don't for - get that God in heav - en an - swers
4. age is steal - ing on, And your bod - y bends be-neath the weight of

1. fare, Just re - mem - ber, in His word, how He
2. spair, Je - sus knows the pain you feel, He can
3. prayer; He will make a way for you and will
4. care; He will nev - er leave you then, He'll go

1. feeds the lit - tle bird;Take your bur - den to the Lord and leave it there.
2. save and He can heal;Take your bur - den to the Lord and leave it there.
3. lead you safe - ly thro';Take your bur - den to the Lord and leave it there.
4. with you to the end;Take your bur - den to the Lord and leave it there.

C. Albert Tindley

Gospel Hymn
Arr. Charles A. Tindley, Jr.

PRAISE

Refrain

Leave it there, _____ leave it there, _____ Take your
Leave it there, leave it there,

bur - den to the Lord and leave it there; _____ If you
leave it there;

trust and nev - er doubt, He will sure - ly bring you out; Take your

bur - den to the Lord and leave it there. _____
leave it there.

PRAISE

91 There Is a Fountain

1. There is a foun - tain filled with blood Drawn
2. The dy - ing thief re - joiced to see That
3. Thou dy - ing Lamb, Thy pre - cious blood Shall
4. E'er since by faith I saw the stream Thy
5. Then in a no - bler, sweet - er song, I'll

1. from Im - man - uel's veins, And sin - ners, plunged be -
2. foun - tain in his day; And there may I, though
3. nev - er lose its pow'r, Till all the ran - somed
4. flow - ing wounds sup - ply, Re - deem - ing love has
5. sing Thy pow'r to save, When this poor, lisp - ing

1. neath that flood, Lose all their guilt - y stains: Lose
2. vile as he, Wash all my sins a - way: Wash
3. Church of God Are saved, to sin no more: Are
4. been my theme, And shall be till I die: And
5. stamm - 'ring tongue Lies si - lent in the grave: Lies

William Cowper

Hymn
Arr. Lowell Mason

PRAISE

1. all their guilt-y stains, Lose all their guilt-y stains; And
2. all my sins a - way, Wash all my sins a - way; And
3. saved, to sin no more, Are saved, to sin no more; Till
4. shall be till I die, And shall be till I die; Re -
5. si - lent in the grave, Lies si - lent in the grave; When

1. sin - ners, plunged be - neath that flood, Lose all their guilt - y stains.
2. there may I, though vile as he, Wash all my sins a - way.
3. all the ran-somed Church of God Are saved, to sin no more.
4. deem - ing love has been my theme, And shall be till I die.
5. this poor lisp - ing, stamm-'ring tongue Lies si - lent in the grave.

92 We're Marching to Zion

1. Come, we that love the Lord, And let our joys be known, Join
2. Let those re - fuse to sing Who nev - er knew our God; But
3. The hill of Zi - on yields A thou-sand sa - cred sweets Be -
4. Then let our songs a-bound, And ev - 'ry tear be dry; We're

1. in a song with sweet ac - cord, Join in a song with sweet ac -
2. chil - dren of the heav'n-ly King, But chil - dren of the heav'n - ly
3. fore we reach the heav'n-ly fields, Be - fore we reach the heav'n - ly
4. march -ing thro' Im - man - uel's ground, We're march-ing thro' Im - man - uel's

1. cord, And thus sur - round the throne, And thus sur-round the throne.
2. King, May speak their joys a-broad, May speak their joys a - broad.
3. fields, Or walk the gold - en streets, Or walk the gold - en streets.
4. ground, To fair - er worlds on high, To fair - er worlds on high.

thus sur-round the throne, And thus sur - round the throne.

Refrain

We're march - ing to Zi - on, Beau - ti-ful, beau - ti - ful
We're march - ing on to Zi - on,

Isaac Watts

Hymn
Robert Lowry

PRAISE

Zi - on; We're march-ing up-ward to Zi - on,
Zi - on, Zi - on,

The beau - ti - ful cit - y of God.

93   Savior, Again to Thy Dear Name We Raise

1. Sav - iour, a - gain to thy dear Name we raise With one ac -
2. Grant us thy peace, Lord, through the com - ing night; Turn thou for
3. Grant us thy peace through - out our earth - ly life; Peace to thy
4. Thy peace in life, the balm of ev - 'ry pain; Thy peace in

1. cord our part - ing hymn of praise; Guard thou the lips from sin, the
2. us its dark - ness in - to light; From harm and dan - ger keep thy
3. Church from er - ror and from strife; Peace to our land, the fruit of
4. death, the hope to rise a - gain; Then, when thy voice shall bid our

1. hearts from shame, That in this house have called up - on thy Name.
2. chil - dren free, For dark and light are both a - like to thee.
3. truth and love; Peace in each heart, thy Spir - it from a - bove:
4. con - flict cease, Call us, O Lord, to thine e - ter - nal peace.

A - men.

John Ellerton

Hymn
Edward J. Hopkins

PRAISE

94 Come by Here

1. Come by here — Lord, come by here, —
2. Some-body needs you Lord, come by here, —
3. Looking for a bless - ing Lord, come by here, —

1. Come by here — Lord, come by here,— Come by here — Lord,
2. Some-body needs you Lord, come by here,— Some-body needs you Lord,
3. Looking for a bless-ing Lord, come by here,— Looking for a bless-ing Lord,

Come by here,— O Lord, come by here. —

Traditional

Spiritual
Arr. Richard Smallwood

PRAYER

95 I Need Thee Every Hour

1. I need Thee ev - 'ry hour, Most gra - cious
2. I need Thee ev - 'ry hour; Stay Thou near
3. I need Thee ev - 'ry hour, In joy or
4. I need Thee ev - 'ry hour; Teach me Thy

1. Lord; No ten - der voice like Thine Can peace af - ford.
2. by; Temp - ta - tions lose their power When Thou art nigh.
3. pain; Come quick - ly and a - bide, Or life is vain.
4. will; And Thy rich prom - is - es In me ful - fill.

Refrain

I need Thee, O I need Thee, Ev - 'ry hour I need Thee; O

bless me now, my Sav - ior, I come to Thee. A - men.

Annie S. Hawks

Hymn
Robert Lowry

PRAYER

96 Pass Me Not, O Gentle Savior

1. Pass me not, O gen - tle Sav - ior, Hear my hum - ble cry;
2. Let me at Thy throne of mer - cy Find a sweet re - lief;
3. Trust - ing on - ly in Thy mer - it, Would I seek Thy face;
4. Thou the spring of all my com - fort, More than life to me,

1. While on oth - ers Thou art call - ing, Do not pass me by.
2. Kneel - ing there in deep con - tri - tion, Help my un - be - lief.
3. Heal my wound-ed, bro-ken spir - it, Save me by Thy grace.
4. Whom have I on earth be - side Thee? Whom in heav'n but Thee?

Refrain

Sav - ior, Sav - ior, Hear my hum - ble cry;

While on oth - ers Thou art call - ing, Do not pass me by.

Fanny J. Crosby

Hymn
William H. Doane

PRAYER

97 Standing in the Need of Prayer

It's me, it's me, O Lord, Stand-ing in the need of pray'r;

Repeat pp
Fine

It's me, it's me, O Lord, Stand-ing in the need of pray'r.

1. Not my broth-er, but it's me, O Lord, Stand-ing in the need of pray'r;
2. Not my sis - ter, but it's me, O Lord, Stand-ing in the need of pray'r;
3. Not my moth-er, but it's me, O Lord, Stand-ing in the need of pray'r;
4. Not my el - der, but it's me, O Lord, Stand-ing in the need of pray'r;

D. C.

1. Not my broth-er, but it's me, O Lord, Stand-ing in the need of pray'r.
2. Not my sis - ter, but it's me, O Lord, Stand-ing in the need of pray'r.
3. Not my moth-er, but it's me, O Lord, Stand-ing in the need of pray'r.
4. Not my el - der, but it's me, O Lord, Stand-ing in the need of pray'r.

Traditional

Spiritual
Arr. John W. Work

Reprinted from AMERICAN NEGRO SONGS AND SPIRITUALS by John W. Work. © 1940, 1968 by Crown Publishers, Inc. By permission of Crown Publishers.

PRAYER

98   I've Just Come from the Fountain

Traditional

Spiritual

SACRAMENTS — BAPTISM

99 Take Me to the Water

1. Take me to the wa - ter, take me to the wa -

ter,__ Take me to the wa - ter to be bap - tized.

2. None but the righteous,
   None but the righteous,
   None but the righteous
   Shall see God.

3. I love Jesus,
   I love Jesus,
   I love Jesus,
   Yes, I do.

4. He's my Saviour,
   He's my Saviour,
   He's my Saviour
   Yes, He is.

Traditional

Spiritual
Arr. Horace Clarence Boyer

SACRAMENTS — BAPTISM

100 Wade in the Water

Wade in the wa-ter, (chil-dren,) Wade in the wa-ter, chil-dren,

Wade in the wa-ter, God's a-going to trou-ble the wa-ter; O wa-ter.

1. See that host all dressed in white, God's a-going to trouble the wa-ter;
2. See that band all dressed in red, God's a-going to trouble the wa-ter;
3. Look o-ver yon-der, what do I see? God's a-going to trouble the wa-ter;
4. If you don't believe I've been re - deemed, God's a-going to trouble the wa-ter;

D. C.

1. The Lead-er looks like the Is - rael-ite, God's a-going to trouble the wa-ter.
2. Looks like the band that Mos - es led, God's a-going to trouble the wa-ter.
3. The Ho - ly Ghost a - com-ing on me, God's a-going to trouble the wa-ter.
4. Just follow me down to Jor-dan's stream, God's a-going to trouble the wa-ter.

Traditional

Spiritual
Arr. Willa A. Townsend

BAPTISM

101 Break Thou the Bread of Life

1. Break Thou the bread of life, Dear Lord, to me,
2. Bless Thou the truth, dear Lord, To me, to me,
3. Teach me to live, dear Lord, On - ly for Thee,

1. As Thou didst break the loaves Be - side the sea;
2. As Thou didst bless the bread By Gal - i - lee;
3. As Thy dis - ci - ples lived in Gal - i - lee;

1. Be - yond the sa - cred page I seek Thee, Lord;
2. Then shall all bond - age cease, All fet - ters fall,
3. Then, all my strug - gles o'er, Then, vic - t'ry won,

1. My spir - it pants for Thee, O liv - ing Word!
2. And I shall find my peace, My All in All.
3. I shall be - hold Thee, Lord, The liv - ing One. A - men.

Mary A. Lathbury

Hymn
William F. Sherwin

EUCHARIST

102 Let Us Break Bread Together

Harmony

1. Let us break bread to - geth - er on our knees, ___
2. Let us drink wine to - geth - er on our knees, ___
3. Let us praise God to - geth - er on our knees, ___

___ Let us break bread to - geth - er on our knees, ___
___ Let us drink wine to - geth - er on our knees, ___
___ Let us praise God to - geth - er on our knees, ___

___ When I fall on my knees, with my face to the ris - ing

sun, O Lord have mer - cy on me, on me.

Traditional   Spiritual

EUCHARIST

103   I Know the Lord Has Laid His Hands on Me

O I know the Lord,_____ I know the Lord,_____

I know the Lord laid His hands on me. O me.

Traditional

Spiritual
Arr. Edward Boatner

ORDINATION

1. O   was - n't   that   a   might - y   day?
2. When   Je - sus   washed your sins   a   -   way,
3. Did   e'er you   see   the   light   be - fore?
4. King   Je - sus,   preach - ing   to   the   poor,

I know the Lord laid His hands on me.

ORDINATION

104　Go Preach My Gospel

1. "Go preach my gos - pel," saith the Lord, "Bid
2. "I'll make my great com - mis - sion known, And
3. "Go heal the sick, go raise the dead, Go
4. "While thus ye fol - low my com - mands, I'm
5. He spake and light shone round His head, On

1. the whole earth my grace re - ceive. Ex - plain to them my
2. ye shall prove my gos - pel true By all the works that
3. cast out dev - ils in my Name. Nor let my proph - ets
4. with you till the world shall end. All pow'r is trust - ed
5. a bright cloud to heav'n He rode. They to the far - thest

1. sa - cred word, Bid them be - lieve, o - bey, and live."
2. I have done, And all the won - ders ye shall do."
3. be a - fraid, Tho' man re - proach, and will blas - pheme."
4. in my hands; I can de - stroy, and can de - fend."
5. na - tion spread The grace of their as - cend - ed God. A - men.

Isaac Watts

Hymn
Thomas Hastings

SACRAMENTS — ORDINATION

105 My Lord, What a Morning

Harmony

My Lord, what a morn-ing, My Lord, what a morn-ing, O

my Lord what a morn-ing, When the stars be-gin to fall.

Unison

1. You'll hear the trum - pet sound,_____
2. You'll hear the sin - ner mourn,_____ To wake the
3. You'll hear the Chris - tian shout,_____

na - tions un - der - ground,_____ Look-ing to my God's right

Harmony

hand, When the stars be - gin to fall. _____

D. C. after each stanza

Traditional

Spiritual

SALVATION

106 Christ the Worker

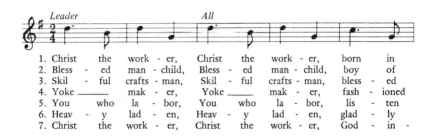

Leader / All

1. Christ	the	work - er,	Christ	the	work - er,	born	in
2. Bless - ed	man - child,	Bless - ed	man - child,	boy	of
3. Skil - ful	crafts - man,	Skil - ful	crafts - man,	bless - ed
4. Yoke ____	mak - er,	Yoke ____	mak - er,	fash - ioned
5. You	who	la - bor,	You	who	la - bor,	lis - ten
6. Heav - y	lad - en,	Heav - y	lad - en,	glad - ly
7. Christ	the	work - er,	Christ	the	work - er,	God - in -

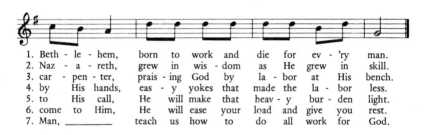

1. Beth - le - hem, born to work and die for ev - 'ry man.
2. Naz - a - reth, grew in wis - dom as He grew in skill.
3. car - pen - ter, prais - ing God by la - bor at His bench.
4. by His hands, eas - y yokes that made the la - bor less.
5. to His call, He will make that heav - y bur - den light.
6. come to Him, He will ease your load and give you rest.
7. Man, _____ teach us how to do all work for God.

Traditional, Ghana

Ghanaian Folk Song
Collected, adapted, translated,
Tom Colvin

SOCIAL JUSTICE

107 Go Down, Moses

Unison

1. When Is-rael was in E-gypt's land, Let my peo-ple go; Op -
2. Thus saith the Lord, bold Mo-ses said, Let my peo-ple go; If

pressed so hard they could not stand, Let my peo-ple go.
not I'll smite your first-born dead, Let my peo-ple go.

Refrain

Go down, Mo-ses, 'Way down in E-gypt's land; __

Tell old __ Pha-raoh Let my peo-ple go.

*Repeat Refrain
after each stanza*

Traditional   Spiritual

SOCIAL JUSTICE

108 In Christ There Is No East or West

1. In Christ there is no East or West, In Him no South or North; But one great fellow-ship of love Throughout the whole wide earth.

2. In Him shall true hearts everywhere Their high communion find; His service is the golden cord Close-binding all mankind.

3. Join hands, then, brothers of the faith, What-e'er your race may be! Who serves my Father as a son Is surely kin to me.

4. In Christ now meet both East and West, In Him meet South and North; All Christly souls are one in him Throughout the whole wide earth.

John Oxenham

Hymn
Adapted, Harry T. Burleigh

SOCIAL JUSTICE

109 Oh, Freedom

Harmony

1. Oh, _____ free-dom, oh, _____ free-dom, oh, _____ free-dom o - ver
2. No more moan-ing, no more moan-ing, no more moan-ing o - ver
3. There'll be sing-ing, there'll be sing-ing, there'll be sing-ing o - ver

me, _____
me, _____ And be - fore I'd be a slave, I'll be
me, _____ o - ver me, And be

bur - ied in my grave, And go home to my Lord, and be free.

Traditional

Spiritual
Arr. Evelyn Davidson White

SOCIAL JUSTICE

110 I Shall Not Be Moved

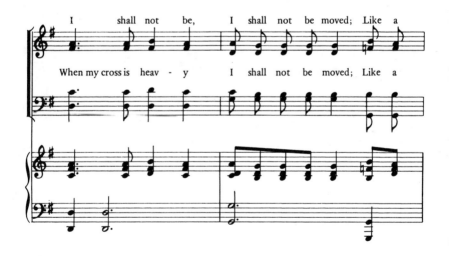

Traditional

Spiritual
Arr. Richard Smallwood

Copyright © Richard Smallwood. Used by permission.

SOCIAL JUSTICE

2. The church of God is marching,
   I shall not be moved.   *Chorus*

3. King Jesus is the Captain,
   I shall not be moved.   *Chorus*

4. Come on and join the army,
   I shall not be moved.   *Chorus*

5. Fighting sin and Satan,
   I shall not be moved.   *Chorus*

6. When my burden's heavy,
   I shall not be moved.   *Chorus*

7. Don't let the world deceive you,
   I shall not be moved.   *Chorus*

8. If my friends forsake me,
   I shall not be moved.   *Chorus*

111   Lift Every Voice and Sing

1. Lift ev - 'ry voice and sing, Till earth and heav - en
2. Sto - ny the road we trod, Bit - ter the chast - 'ning
3. God of our wea - ry years, God of our si - lent

James Weldon Johnson

Anthem
J. Rosamond Johnson

SOCIAL JUSTICE

1. ring, Ring with the har - mo - nies of Lib - er -
2. rod, Felt in the days when hope un - born had
3. tears, Thou who hast brought us thus far on the

1. ty; Let our re - joic - ing rise High as the list - 'ning
2. died; Yet with a stead - y beat, Have not our wear - y
3. way; Thou who hast by Thy might, Led us in - to the

1. skies, Let it re - sound loud as the roll - ing sea.
2. feet Come to the place for which our fa - thers sighed?
3. light, Keep us for - ev - er in the path, we pray.

SOCIAL JUSTICE

1. Sing a song full of the faith that the dark past has taught us
2. We have come o-ver a - way that with tears has been wa - tered
3. Lest our feet stray from the pla-ces,our God,where we met Thee,

1. Sing a song full of the hope that the pres-ent has
2. We have come, tread-ing our path thro' the blood of the
3. Lest our hearts, drunk with the wine of the world, we for -

SOCIAL JUSTICE

1. brought us; Fac-ing the ris - ing sun Of our new
2. slaugh - tered; Out from the gloom - y past, Till now we
3. get Thee; Shad-owed be-neath Thy hand, May we for -

1. day be - gun, Let us march on till vic-to - ry is won.
2. stand at last Where the white gleam of our bright star is cast.
3. ev - er stand, True to our God, True to our na - tive land.

SOCIAL JUSTICE

112 Mine Eyes Have Seen the Glory

Julia Ward Howe

Hymn
William Steffe
Arr. Horace Clarence Boyer

SOCIAL JUSTICE

Refrain

Glo - ry, glo - ry, hal - le - lu - jah!

Glo - ry, glo - ry, hal - le - lu - jah! Glo - ry, glo - ry, hal - le -

lu - jah! His truth is march - ing on.

2. I have seen Him in the watchfires of a hundred circling camps;
   They have builded Him an altar in the evening dews and damps;
   I can read His righteous sentence by the dim and flaring lamps;
   His day is marching on. *Refrain*

3. He has sounded forth the trumpet that shall never sound retreat;
   He is sifting out the hearts of men before His judgment seat.
   O be swift, my soul, to answer Him! be jubilant, my feet!
   Our God is marching on. *Refrain*

4. In the beauty of the lilies, Christ was born across the sea,
   With a glory in His bosom that transfigures you and me;
   As He died to make men holy, let us die to make men free;
   While God is marching on. *Refrain*

SOCIAL JUSTICE

113   We Shall Overcome

Moderately slow with determination (♩ = 66)

1. We shall o - ver - come,___ We shall o - ver - come,___
2. We'll walk hand in hand,___ We'll walk hand in hand,___

1. We shall o - ver - come some day,___
2. We'll walk hand in hand some day,___

1. ___ Oh,___ deep in my heart
2. ___ Oh,___ deep in my heart

Traditional

Freedom Song
Arr. Richard Smallwood

SOCIAL JUSTICE

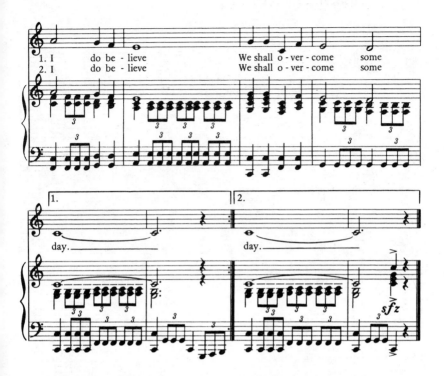

1. I do be - lieve We shall o - ver - come some
2. I do be - lieve We shall o - ver - come some

1.
day._____

2.
day._____

3. We are not afraid,
   we are not afraid,
   We are not afraid today,
   Oh, deep in my heart I do believe
   We shall overcome some day.

4. We shall stand together,
   we shall stand together,
   We shall stand together—now,
   Oh deep in my heart I do believe
   We shall overcome some day.

5. The truth will make us free,
   the truth will make us free,
   The truth will make us free some day.
   Oh, deep in my heart I do believe
   We shall overcome some day.

6. The Lord will see us through,
   the Lord will see us through,
   The Lord will see us through some day.
   Oh, deep in my heart I do believe
   We shall overcome some day.

7. We shall be like Him,
   we shall be like Him,
   We shall be like Him someday,
   Oh, deep in my heart I do believe
   We shall overcome some day.

8. We shall live in peace,
   we shall live in peace,
   We shall live in peace some day
   Oh, deep in my heart I do believe
   We shall overcome some day.

9. The whole wide world around,
   the whole wide world around,
   The whole wide world around some day,
   Oh, deep in my heart I do believe
   We shall overcome some day.

10. We shall overcome,
    we shall overcome,
    We shall overcome some day,
    Oh, deep in my heart I do believe
    We shall overcome some day.

SOCIAL JUSTICE

114   Amazing Grace

John Newton

Gospel Hymn
Arr. Richard Smallwood

WITNESS

115 Faith of Our Fathers

1. Faith of our fa - thers! liv - ing still In spite of dun - geon,
2. Our fa - thers, chained in pris - ons dark, Were still in heart and
3. Faith of our fa - thers! faith and prayer Shall win all na - tions
4. Faith of our fa - thers! we will love Both friend and foe in

1. fire, and sword: O how our hearts beat high with joy,
2. con - science free: And tru - ly blest would be our fate,
3. un - to thee; And through the truth that comes from God,
4. all our strife: And preach thee, too, as love knows how,

Refrain

1. When - e'er we hear that glo - rious word:
2. If we, like them, should die for thee.   Faith of our fa - thers,
3. Man - kind shall then in - deed be free.
4. By kind - ly deeds and vir - tuous life.

ho - ly faith, We will be true to thee till death.

Frederick W. Faber

Hymn
Henri F. Hemy

WITNESS

116　Beams of Heaven (Some Day)

1. Beams of heav - en, as I go, Thro' this wil - der - ness be -
2. Oft - en times my sky is clear, Joy a - bounds with-out a
3. Hard - er yet may be the fight, Right may oft - en yield to
4. Bur - dens now may crush me down, Dis - ap - point - ments all a -

1. low. Guide my feet in peace - ful ways, Turn my
2. tear, Though a day so bright be - gun, Clouds may
3. might, Wick - ed - ness a - while may reign, Sa - tan's
4. round. Trou - bles speak in mourn - ful sigh, Sor - row

1. mid - nights in - to days; When in the dark - ness I would
2. hide to - mor-row's sun. There'll be a day that's al - ways
3. cause may seem to gain, There is a God that rules a -
4. thro' a tear - stain'd eye. There is a world where pleas - ure

1. grope, Faith al - ways sees a star of hope. And soon from
2. bright, A day that nev - er yields to night, And in its
3. bove, With hand of pow'r and heart of love; If I am
4. reigns, No mourn - ing soul shall roam its plains, And to that

Charles A. Tindley

Hymn
Arr. F. A. Clark

WITNESS

1. all   life's grief and   dan - ger,   I shall be   free   some   day,
2. light   the streets of   glo - ry   I shall be - hold   some   day.
3. right,   He'll fight my   bat - tle,   I shall have peace   some   day.
4. land   of peace and   glo - ry   I want to   go,   some   day.

Refrain

I do not   know how long 'twill be,   nor what the   fu - ture holds for

me, But this I   know, if Je - sus leads me,   I shall get   home   some   day.

WITNESS

117 Give Me Jesus

Harmony

1. In the morn-ing when I rise, In the morn-ing when I rise, In the morn-ing when I rise, Give me Je - sus.
2. Dark __ mid - night was my cry, Dark __ mid - night was my cry, Dark __ mid - night was my cry, Give me Je - sus.
3. O __ when I come to die, O __ when I come to die, O __ when I come to die Give me Je - sus.

Give me Je - sus, Give me Je - sus, You may have all this world, Give me Je - sus.

Traditional

Spiritual
Arr. Evelyn Davidson White

Used by permission.

WITNESS

118   Lord, I Want to Be a Christian

1. Lord, I want to be a Chris-tian In my heart, in my heart;
2. Lord, I want to be more lov-ing In my heart, in my heart;
3. Lord, I want to be more ho-ly In my heart, in my heart;
4. I don't want to be like Ju-das In my heart, in my heart;
5. Lord, I want to be like Je-sus In my heart, in my heart;

1. Lord, I want to be a Chris-tian In my heart,
2. Lord, I want to be more lov-ing In my heart,
3. Lord, I want to be more ho-ly In my heart,
4. I don't want to be like Ju-das In my heart,
5. Lord, I want to be like Je-sus In my heart,

In my heart,   In my heart,

1. Lord, I want to be a Chris-tian In my heart.
2. Lord, I want to be more lov-ing In my heart.
3. Lord, I want to be more ho-ly In my heart.
4. I don't want to be like Ju-das In my heart.
5. Lord, I want to be like Je-sus In my heart.

Traditional

Spiritual
Arr. Edward C. Deas

WITNESS

119   I Love To Tell the Story

1. I love to tell the sto - ry Of un - seen things a - bove,
2. I love to tell the sto - ry, For those who know it best

Of Je - sus and is glo - ry, Of Je - sus and His love.
Seem hun - ger-ing and thirst-ing To hear it, like the rest.

I love to tell the sto - ry, Be - cause I know it's true;
And when, in scenes of glo - ry, I sing the new, new song,

It sat - is-fies my long-ings As noth - ing else would do.
'Twill be the old, old sto - ry That I have loved so long.

Refrain

I love to tell the sto - ry; 'Twill be my theme in glo - ry

Katherine Hankey

Hymn
William G. Fischer

WITNESS

To tell the old, old sto-ry Of Je-sus and His love.

120   Have You Got Good Religion? (Certainly, Lord)

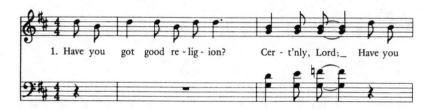

1. Have you got good re-lig-ion? Cer-t'nly, Lord;_ Have you

got good re-lig-ion? Cer-t'nly, Lord;_ Have you got good re-lig-ion?

Cer-t'nly, Lord, _____ Cer-t'nly, cer-t'nly,_ cer-t'nly, Lord._

2. Have you been redeemed?
3. Have you been to the water?
4. Have you been baptized?
5. Is your name on high?
6. Has your name been changed?

Traditional

Spiritual
Arr. Edward Boatner

WITNESS

121 I Am Thine, O Lord

1. I am Thine, O Lord, I have heard Thy voice, And it
2. Con - se - crate me now to Thy ser - vice, Lord, By the
3. Oh, the pure de - light of a sin gle hour That be -
4. There are depths of love that I can - not know Till I

1. told Thy love to me; But I long to rise in the
2. pow'r of grace di - vine; Let my soul look up with a
3. fore Thy throne I spend, When I kneel in prayer, and with
4. cross the nar - row sea; There are heights of joy that I

1. arms of faith, And be clos - er drawn to Thee.
2. stead - fast hope, And my will be lost in Thine.
3. Thee, my God, I com - mune as friend with friend!
4. may not reach Till I rest in peace with Thee.

Fanny Crosby

Hymn
William H. Doane

WITNESS

Refrain

Draw me near - - er, near - er, bless-ed Lord, To the

near - er, near - er,

cross where Thou hast died; Draw me near - er, near - er,

near-er, bless-ed Lord, To Thy pre-cious, bleed - ing side.

WITNESS

122　This Little Light of Mine

1. This lit - tle light of mine I'm gon-na let it shine, *

Oh __　　　　　　　　Oh __

This lit - tle light of mine I'm gon-na let it shine;

This lit - tle light of mine I'm gon - na let it

shine, Let it shine, let it shine, let it shine. _____

* Gonna may be changed to "going to."

Traditional

Spiritual
Arr. Horace Clarence Boyer

WITNESS

2. Ev'ry where I go, I'm gonna let it shine,
   Ev'ry where I go, I'm gonna let it shine;
   Ev'ry where I go, I'm gonna let it shine,
   Let it shine, let it shine, let it shine.

3. Jesus gave it to me, I'm gonna let it shine,
   Jesus gave it to me, I'm gonna let it shine;
   Jesus gave it to me, I'm gonna let it shine,
   Let it shine, let it shine, let it shine.

123   We Are Climbing Jacob's Ladder

1. We are climb-ing Ja-cob's lad-der, We are
2. Ev-'ry round goes high-er, high-er, Ev-'ry
3. Sin-ner do you love my Je-sus, Sin-ner
4. If you love Him why not serve Him, If you

climb-ing Ja-cob's lad-der, We are climb-ing
round goes high-er, high-er, Ev-'ry round goes
do you love my Je-sus, Sin-ner do you
love Him why not serve Him, If you love Him

Ja-cob's lad-der, Sol-diers of the cross.
high-er, high-er, Sol-diers of the cross.
love my Je-sus, Sol-diers of the cross.
why not serve Him, Sol-diers of the cross.

Traditional

Spiritual

WITNESS

124   Where Cross the Crowded Ways of Life

1. Where cross the crowd-ed ways of life, Where sound the
   cries of race and clan, A - bove the noise of self - ish
   strife, We hear thy voice, O Son of man.

2. In haunts of wretch-ed - ness and need, On shad-owed
   thresh-olds dark with fears, From paths where hide the lures of
   greed, We catch the vi - sion of thy tears.

3. From ten - der child-hood's help - less - ness, From wom-an's
   grief, man's bur - den'd toil, From fam-ished souls, from sor-row's
   stress, Thy heart hath nev - er known re - coil. A - men.

4. The cup of water giv'n for thee
   Still holds the freshness of thy grace;
   Yet long these multitudes to see
   The sweet compassion of thy face.

5. O Master, from the mountain side,
   Make haste to heal these hearts of pain;
   Among these restless throngs abide,
   O tread the city's streets again.

6. Till sons of men shall learn thy love,
   And follow where thy feet have trod;
   Till glorious from thy heav'n above,
   Shall come the city of our God. Amen.

F. M. North

Hymn
W. Gardiner

WITNESS

125   Where He Leads Me

1. I can hear my Sav - ior call - ing, I can hear my Sav - ior call - ing,
2. I'll go with Him thro' the gar-den, I'll go with Him thro' the gar - den,
3. I'll go with Him thro' the judg-ment, I'll go with Him thro' the judg - ment,
4. He will give me grace and glo - ry, He will give me grace and glo - ry,

1. I can hear my Sav - ior call - ing, "Take thy cross and fol-low, fol - low me."
2. I'll go with Him thro' the gar - den. I'll go with Him, with Him all the way.
3. I'll go with Him thro' the judg-ment, I'll go with Him, with Him all the way.
4. He will give me grace and glo - ry, And go with me, with me all the way.

Refrain

Where He leads me I will fol-low, Where He leads me I will fol-low,

Where He leads me I will fol-low, I'll go with Him, with Him all the way.

E. W. Blandy

Hymn
J. S. Norris

WITNESS

126 Yes, God Is Real

1. There are some things I may not know, There are some plac - es I can't go, ____ But I am sure of this one thing ____ That God is real, for I can feel Him deep with - in.

Refrain

Yes, God is real, ____ real in my

Kenneth Morris

Gospel
Kenneth Morris
Arr. Horace Clarence Boyer

2. Some folk may doubt, some folk may scorn
   All can desert and leave me alone;
   But as for me I'll take God's part
   For God is real and I can feel Him in my heart.

3. I cannot tell just how you felt
   When Jesus took your sins away;
   But since that day, yes, since that hour
   God has been real for I can feel His holy pow'r.

WITNESS

Opening Preces Morning Prayer II

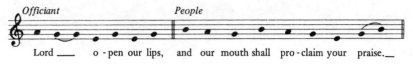

Officiant   *People*

Lord ___ o - pen our lips,   and our mouth shall pro - claim your praise.__

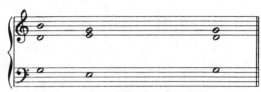

Officiant and People

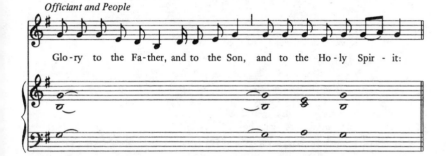

Glo - ry to the Fa - ther, and to the Son,   and to the Ho - ly Spir - it:

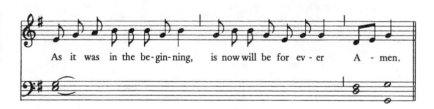

As it was in the be - gin - ning,   is now will be for ev - er   A - men.

Except in Lent

Al - le - lu - ia.

William B. Cooper

Copyright © William B. Cooper. Used by permission.

LITURGICAL

128 Venite

1. Come, let us˘sing to the˘Lord;*
   let us shout for joy to the˘Rock of˘our sal˘vation.

2. Let us come before his˘presence with˘thanksgiving*
   and raise a loud˘shout to˘him with˘psalms.   [Ant.]

3. For the Lord is a˘great˘God,*
   and a great˘King a˘bove all˘gods.

4. In his hand are the˘caverns of the˘earth,*
   and the heights of the˘hills are˘his˘also.

†5. The sea is˘his, for he˘made it,*
    and his hands have˘molded the˘dry˘land.   [Ant.]

† *Second half of double chant.*

6. Come, let us bow down, and˘bend the˘knee,*
   and˘kneel before the˘Lord our˘Maker.

7. For he is our God,
   and we are the people of his pasture and the˘sheep of his˘hand.*
   Oh, that to˘day you would˘hearken to his˘voice!   [Ant.]

Venite ends here.

William B. Cooper

LITURGICAL

Psalm 95 continues:

8. Harden not your hearts,
   as your forebears 'did in the 'wilderness,*
      at Méribah, and on that day at 'Massah, 'when they 'tempted me.

9. They 'put me to the 'test,
      ____ 'though they had 'seen my 'works.   [Ant.]

10. Forty years long I detested that gene 'ration and 'said,*
      "This people are wayward in their hearts;
      'they do not 'know my 'ways."

11. So I 'swore in my 'wrath,*
      "They shall not 'enter 'into my 'rest."   [Ant.]

The Gloria may be added when desired.

Glory to the Father, and 'to the 'Son,*
   and 'to the 'Holy 'Spirit:
As it was in the be 'ginning, is 'now,*
   and 'will be for 'ever. A 'men.   [Ant.]

129   Jubilate

A.

B.

1. Be joyful in the 'Lord, all you 'lands;*
   serve the Lord with gladness
   and come before his 'presence 'with a 'song.   [Ant.]

2. Know this: The Lord him 'self is 'God;*
   he himself has made us, and we are his;
   we are his 'people and the 'sheep of his 'pasture.   [Ant.]

3. Enter his gates with thanksgiving;
   go into his 'courts with 'praise;*
   give thanks to 'him and 'call upon his 'Name.   [Ant.]

4. For the Lord is good;
   his mercy is 'ever 'lasting;*
   and his faithfulness en 'dures from 'age to 'age.   [Ant.]

   The Gloria may be added when desired

   Glory to the Father, and 'to the 'Son,*
   and 'to the 'Holy 'Spirit:
   As it was in the be 'ginning, is 'now,*
   and 'will be for 'ever. A 'men.   [Ant.]

William B. Cooper

LITURGICAL

130   Christ Our Passover

1. Alleluia.
   Christ our Passover has been ˈsacrificed forˈus;*
      thereforeˈlet usˈkeep theˈfeast,

2. Not with the old leaven, the leaven ofˈmalice andˈevil,*
      but with the unleavened bread of sinˈcerity andˈtruth. Alleˈluia.

3. Christ being raised from the dead will neverˈdie aˈgain;*
      death noˈlonger has doˈminionˈover him.

4. The death that he died, he died to sin,ˈonce forˈall;*
      but the life heˈlives, heˈlives toˈGod.

5. So also consider yourselvesˈdead toˈsin,*
      and alive to God in JesusˈChrist ourˈLord. Alleˈluia.

6. Christ has beenˈraised from theˈdead,*
      the first fruits ofˈthose who haveˈfallen aˈsleep.

7. For since by aˈman cameˈdeath,*
      by a man has come also the resurˈrectionˈof theˈdead.

8. For as inˈAdam allˈdie,*
      so also in Christ shall all beˈmade aˈlive. Alleˈluia.

   The Gloria may be added when desired

   Glory to the Father, andˈto theˈSon,*
      andˈto theˈHolyˈSpirit:
   As it was in the beˈginning, isˈnow,*
      and will be forˈever. Aˈmen. Alleˈluia.

William B. Cooper

LITURGICAL

131 A Song of Creation

*One or more sections of this Canticle may be used. Whatever the selection,
it begins with the Invocation and concludes with Doxology.*

I. Invocation

1. Glorify the Lord, all you works of the Lord,*
   praise him and highly ex alt him for ever.

2. In the firmament of his power, glorify the Lord,*
   praise him and highly ex alt him for ever.

II. The Cosmic Order

William B. Cooper

LITURGICAL

3. Glorify the Lord, you angels and all'powers of the'Lord,*
   O heavens and all'waters a'bove the'heavens.

4. Sun and moon and stars of the sky,'glorify the'Lord,*
   praise him and'highly ex'alt him for'ever.

5. Glorify the Lord, every shower of rain and'fall of'dew,*
   all'winds and'fire and'heat.

6. Winter and summer,'glorify the'Lord,*
   praise him and'highly ex'alt him for'ever.

7. Glorify the Lord, O'chill and'cold,*
   drops of'dew and'flakes of'snow.

8. Frost and cold, ice and sleet,'glorify the'Lord,*
   praise him and'highly ex'alt him for'ever.

9. Glorify the Lord, O'nights and'days,*
   O shining'light and en'folding'dark.

10. Storm clouds and thunderbolts,'glorify the'Lord,*

III The Earth And Its Creatures

11. Let the earth'glorify the'Lord,*
    praise him and'highly ex'alt him for'ever.

12. Glorify the Lord, O mountains and hills,
    and all that'grows upon the'earth,*
    praise him and'highly ex'alt him for'ever.

13. Glorify the Lord, O springs of water,'seas, and'streams,*
    O whales and'all that'move in the'waters.

14. All birds of the air,'glorify the'Lord,*
    praise him and'highly ex'alt him for'ever.

15. Glorify the Lord, O'beasts of the'wild,*
    and'all you'flocks and'herds.

16. O men and women everywhere,'glorify the'Lord,*
    praise him and'highly ex'alt him for'ever.

III. The People Of God

17. Let the people of God glorify the Lord,*
    praise him and highly ex alt him for ever.

18. Glorify the Lord, O priests and servants of the Lord,*
    praise him and highly ex alt him for ever.

19. Glorify the Lord, O spirits and souls of the righteous,*
    praise him and highly ex alt him for ever,

20. You that are holy and humble of heart, glorify the Lord,*
    praise him and highly ex alt him for ever.

Doxology

21. Let us glorify the Lord: Father, Son, and Holy Spirit;*
    praise him and highly ex alt him for ever.

22. In the firmament of his power, glorify the Lord,*
    praise him and highly ex alt him for ever.

132   The Song of Mary

Magnificat II.

My soul pro - claims the great - ness of the Lord,

my spir - it re - joic - es in God my Sav - iour;

for he has looked with fa - vor on his low - ly ser - vant.

(opt.)   5

From this day all gen - er - a - tions will call me blessed:

the Al - might - y has done great things for me,

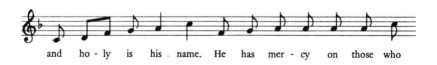

and ho - ly is his . name. He has mer - cy on those who

William B. Cooper

LITURGICAL

fear him in ev - ery gen - er - a - tion. He has shown the strength of his arm,

he has scat - tered the proud in their con - ceit.

He has cast down the might - y from their thrones,

and has lift - ed__ up the low - ly. He has filled the

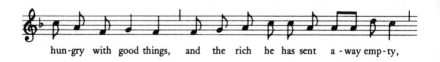

hun-gry with good things, and the rich he has sent a - way emp-ty,

He has come to the help of his ser - vant Is - ra - el,

For he has re - mem - bered his prom - ise of mer - cy,

the prom - ise he made to our fa - thers, to A - bra - ham,

and his chil - dren for ev - er. Glo - ry to the Fa - ther,

and to the Son, and to the Ho - ly Spir - it, as it was in the be - gin - ning,

is now, and will be for ev - er, A - men.

133   A Song of Penitence

Prayer of Manasseh

1. O Lord and Ruler of the hosts of heaven,*
   God of Abraham, Isaac, and Jacob,
   and of all their righteous offspring:

2. You made the heavens and the earth,*
   with all their vast array.

3. All things quake with fear at your presence;*
   they tremble because of your power.

4. But your merciful promise is beyond all measure;*
   it surpasses all that our minds can fathom.

5. O Lord, you are full of compassion,*
   long-suffering, and abounding in mercy.

6. You hold back your hand;*
   you do not punish as we deserve.

7. In your great goodness, Lord,
   you have promised forgiveness to sinners,*
   that they may repent of their sin and be saved.

8. And now, O Lord, I bend the knee of my heart,*
   and make my appeal, sure of your gracious goodness.

9. I have sinned, O Lord, I have sinned,*
   and I know my wickedness only too well.

10. Therefore I make this prayer to you:*
    Forgive me, Lord, forgive me.

11. Do not let me perish in my sin,*
    nor condemn me to the depths of the earth.

William B. Cooper

LITURGICAL

12. For you, O Lord, are the God of those who re'pent,*
    and in me'you will show'forth your'goodness.

13. Unworthy as I am, you will save me,
    in accordance with your'great'mercy,*
    and I will praise you without'ceasing all the'days of my'life.

14. For all the powers of heaven'sing your'praises,*
    and yours is the glory to'ages of'ages. A'men.

134   O Gracious Light

1. O gracious Light,
   pure brightness of the everliving'Father in'heaven,*
   O Jesus'Christ, holy and'blessed!

2. Now as we come to the setting of the sun,
   and our eyes behold the'vesper'light,*
   we sing *your* praises, O God: Father, Son, and'Holy'Spirit.

3. *You are* worthy at all times to be praised by'happy'voices,*
   O Son of God, O Giver of life,
   and to be'glorified through'all the'worlds.

William B. Cooper

LITURGICAL

135 Lord, Have Mercy

(In Unison)

Lord, have mer - cy, Christ, have mer - cy, Lord, have mer - cy.

136 Kyrie Eleison

Ky - ri - e 'e - le - i - son, Chri - ste, e - le - i - son, Ky - ri - e e - le - i - son.

135–142 Cooper Mass

William B. Cooper

Copyright © 1973. DANGERFIELD MUSIC CO., 26 Knickerbocker Road, Englewood, NJ 07631.
Used by permission.

LITURGICAL

137 Holy God

(In Unison)

Ho - ly God, Holy and might - y, Ho-ly Im-mor-tal One. Have mer-cy up - on us, Have mer-cy up - on us, Have mer-cy up - on us.

138   Glory to God (a)

Lord God, Lamb of God, You take a-way the sins of the world,

Have mer-cy on us, You are seat-ed at the right hand of the

Fa-ther, Re - ceive our prayer. For you a - lone are the Lord.___
(con moto)

poco   a

(Ped. sempre legato e coll' voce)

You a - lone are the most high Je - sus Christ with the Ho - ly Spir - it

poco   crescendo   -   -   -

in the glo - ry of God the Fa - ther, ' A - men.

139   Glory to God (b)

Priest

Glo-ry to God in the high - est.

Choir and Congregation
And peace to his peo-ple on

earth. Lord God, Heav - en - ly King, Al -might-y God and Fa - ther.

We wor - ship you, we give you thanks, we praise you for your

glo - ry. Lord Je - sus Christ, on - ly Son of the Fa - ther,

Lord God, Lamb of God, You take a - way the sins of the world,

140 Holy, Holy, Holy, Lord

141   Christ Our Passover

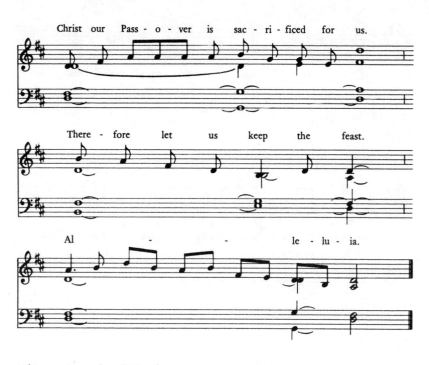

Christ our Pass - o - ver is sac - ri - ficed for us.

There - fore let us keep the feast.

Al - le - lu - ia.

142   Lamb of God

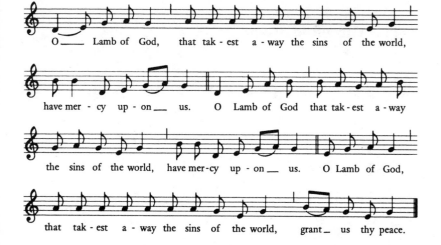

O__ Lamb of God, that tak - est a - way the sins of the world,

have mer - cy up - on__ us. O Lamb of God that tak - est a - way

the sins of the world, have mer - cy up - on__ us. O Lamb of God,

that tak - est a - way the sins of the world, grant__ us thy peace.

143 Hear Our Prayer

Hear our prayer, O Lord, Hear our prayer, O Lord; In-
cline thine ear to us, And grant us thy peace. A - men.

Traditional

George Whelpton
Arr. Horace Clarence Boyer

144 Threefold Amen

A - men, A - men, A - men.

Traditional
Arr. Horace Clarence Boyer

145   Lord Have Mercy

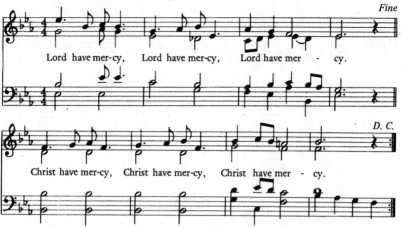

Lord have mer-cy, Lord have mer-cy, Lord have mer - cy.

Christ have mer-cy, Christ have mer-cy, Christ have mer - cy.

146   Glory to God

Glo - ry to God in the high - est and peace to His peo - ple on earth. Lord God, heav - en - ly King, Al - might - y God and Fa - ther,

145–151 Gibson Mass
Used by permission.

Timothy Gibson

LITURGICAL

193

seat - ed at the right hand of the Fa - ther Re -
ceive our prayer For You a - lone are the
Ho - ly One, You a - lone are the Lord; You a -
lone are the Most High Je - sus Christ with the Ho - ly Spir-it in the
glo - ry of God the Fa - ther. A - men.

147 The Creed

We be - lieve   in one God, the   Fa - ther, the Al - might - y
Mak - er of heav-en and   earth   And of   all   that   is,
seen   and   un - seen.   We be - lieve   in one Lord
Je - sus Christ the   on - ly Son   of   God   e -

ter - nal - ly be - got - ten of the Fa - ther God from God, Light from Light, True God from True God, be - got - ten not made Of one be-ing with the Fa - ther thro' Him all things were made. For us men and for our sal - va - tion He came down from heav - en By the

rose a - gain in ac - cord - ance with the scrip - tures He as - cend - ed in - to heav - en and is seat - ed at the right hand of the Fa - ther. He will come a - gain with glo - ry to judge the liv - ing and the dead,

and His king - dom will have no end.

We be - lieve in the Ho - ly Spir - it, The

Lord, the Giv - er of Life who pro - ceeds from the

Fa - ther and the Son, with the Fa - ther and the

Son He is wor - shipped and glo-ri-fied He has spo - ken

through the proph-ets. _____ We be-lieve in one Ho-ly cath-o-lic and Ap-os-tol-ic Church. We ac-knowl-edge one bap-ti-sm for the for-give-ness of sin We look for the res-ur-rec-tion of the dead ___ And the life of the world to come. A - men.

148   Blessing and Honor

Bless - ing   and   hon - our   and   glo - ry   and   pow - er   be   yours   for - ev - er   and _ ev - er.   A - men.

149   Holy, Holy, Holy Lord

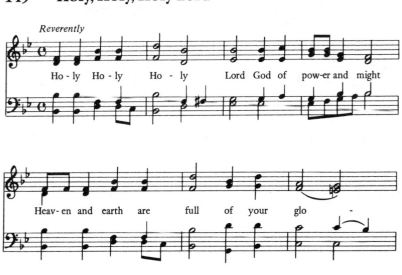

Reverently

Ho - ly   Ho - ly   Ho - ly   Lord God of   pow-er and might   Heav - en and earth   are   full   of   your   glo -

ry. Ho - san - na in the high - est.

Bless - ed is He who comes in the Name of the

Lord. Ho - san - na in the high - est!

150   The Acclamation

Christ has died. Christ is ris - en. Christ will come a - gain.

151 The Lamb of God

Lamb of God, you take a - way the sin of the world, Lamb of

God, you take a - way the sin of the world; Lamb of

God, you take a - way the sin of the world, have

1. mer-cy on us.

2. Grant us your peace.

Music Among Blacks in the
Episcopal Church:
Some Preliminary Considerations

Irene V. Jackson

This essay examines historically the musical activities of blacks in the Episcopal church.

To date, scholarly attention has been given primarily to the religious experience of blacks who were outside mainline denominations. One is hard-pressed to find adequate discussion of black *religious* activities within the principal churches of America. The situation becomes even more critical when the subject is the *musical* activities of black people in the larger religious bodies. It is not the intent of this essay to offer an explanation of the paucity of material on black, musical practices in mainline denominations. Rather the attention of this study is given to the musical activities of blacks in the Episcopal church. An analysis of the social forces which gave rise to black musical attitudes is an important subject. However, a socio-historical examination of the musical activities of black Episcopalians will be left for another time.

The larger issue that will be addressed in the course of this essay is the religious musical tradition of Afro-Americans.

Scholarly interest in the religious music of Afro-Americans has been almost exclusively devoted to the study of one genre — the spiritual — and of musical activities among black independent denominations where worship modes are covertly or overtly linked to West African modes.

The account of the English musician Henry Russell who visited the United States from 1833 to 1841 is representative of accounts of black worship patterns. Russell writes:

> "I had long taken a deep interest in Negro life, and I wondered whether it was possible that Negroes could originate melody. I was desirous of testing this, and I made up my mind to visit many Negro meetings throughout several of the states. On my entering the chapel at Vicksburg [then a slave town] there was a restlessness about the little congregation — whether it emanated from one or two white people being present I cannot say. There was one peculiarity that struck me forcible. When the minister gave out his own version of the Psalm, the choir commenced singing so rapidly that the original tune absolutely ceased to exist — in fact, the fine old psalm tune became thoroughly transformed. For a moment, I fancied that not only the choir but the little congregation intended to get up a dance as part of the service."[1]

The above description is but one example of the many recorded accounts of black worship

Reprinted with permission of the Historical Society of the Episcopal Church

patterns. However, these accounts focus primarily on situations that involve the more demonstrative forms of religious behaviour such as shouting, dancing, or glossolalia.

The religious music of Afro-Americans must be thoroughly investigated and perceptively conceptualized. Therefore, a discussion of religious music of Afro-Americans — as this essay intends to show — must take into account not only music in black independent churches but also the musical practices of blacks in mainline denominations.

It will be demonstrated that blacks in the Episcopal church have historically regarded music as central to their Christian lives.

Music and the Ante-Bellum Church

The history of musical practices among black Episcopalians in a formal way begins in the latter part of the eighteenth century in Philadelphia with Absalom Jones and Richard Allen, who together formed "The Free African Society." Jones went on to found the first black Episcopal parish in the United States — St. Thomas African Episcopal Church — which was established in 1794 in Philadelphia. The minutes of the January 18, 1793 meeting of the "Free African Society," which was attended by Absalom Jones, give the first glimpse of attitudes about music within the "Society." Since Jones was present at the meeting and presumably voted on the "recommended rules" of the "Society," we have some idea about his attitudes regarding music in worship. From the minutes of this meeting, "it was recommended that at the time of singing, the *congregation* shall stand or keep seated as *they* find freedom, and that the *congregation* should supply such books as are necessary to read, *sing,* and praise the Lord in harmony."[2] We know then that music was an integral part of worship and that *congregational* singing was encouraged. We know also from the minutes that singing should be entered into as a *corporate* act of worship.

In a somewhat less formal sense the history of music among black Episcopalians begins in the early eighteenth century with the work of the Society for the Propagation of the Gospel in Foreign Parts which consisted of English missionaries who were sent to the Colonies to Christianize blacks and Indians.

The early work of the S. P. G. took place in Goose Creek, South Carolina where slaves were reported to have been converted in 1695 under the Rev. Samuel Thomas. From 1712, the work of the S. P. G. was spearheaded by the Rev. George Ross who, as a missionary, put forth an effort to provide slaves with instruction in church Catechism. His efforts were largely concentrated in Delaware. Ross, in a letter to the S. P. G., indicated that the Quakers gave little attention to instructing slaves and that the few slaves who were baptized belonged to Churchmen, that is Anglicans. Probably the most important and well-known name in connection with the S. P. G. was the Rev. Thomas Bray. An early eighteenth century letter to the S. P. G. from a clergyman, a missionary who served in St. James parish in South Carolina, reported that the work among the blacks was successful because the Lord's Day was no longer profaned by dancing. One of the conditions of baptism as set down by the white clergymen was that slaves were required to promise that they would not spend the Lord's Day in feasts, dances and merry meetings.[3]

In addition to being instructed in the church Catechism, blacks were introduced to the music of the Anglican Church in the way of singing the psalms, as reported by a New York clergyman to the Society in a letter dated December 3, 1726.[4] Missionary activity was moving along full-tilt in Savannah, Georgia and Charleston, South Carolina by the 1730's and missionaries requested that the S. P. G. send "Bibles, primers, spelling books, hornbooks, testaments and *psalters.*"[5] Blacks were taught to sing psalms using a practice referred to as "lining-out." The song leader or precentor would sing one or two lines of the psalm and the congregation followed, repeating the lines with some melodic ornamentation. The practice of "lining-out" was a device used to teach slaves to read and sing from notes.

Contrary to the popularly held notion that blacks were not attracted to the formality of Anglican worship style, we learn from letters dated September 30, 1745 and March 28, 1751 and sent to the S. P. G. from missionaries in New York that "the singing of a psalm had produced a good effect: it had engaged many of the Negroes to a closer application in learning to read," and "that blacks often meet in the evenings on a regular basis for instruction in the singing of the psalm tunes."[6] It seems reasonable to assume from the aforementioned quotes that music was used by blacks non-liturgically, as a means of providing group solidarity and identity.

Where blacks worshipped along with whites, although most often restricted to a special area, or where blacks worshipped in a separate building under white leadership, blacks were, by the founding of black independent churches in the late eighteenth century, beginning to experience musical syncretism within the colonial Church of England. That is, blacks were fusing certain African and Afro-American musical practices with Anglo-American musical practices.

In a history of black Episcopalians, Robert Bennett suggests how this musical syncretism manifested itself. Bennett writes:

> "In the south, where the majority of black Episcopalians were to be found and where prior to the Civil War the Bishop of South Carolina claimed more black communicants than white and where black churchmen worshipped in separate galleries or chapels, it was this body which described their plantation Holy Communion services in the spiritual, "Let Us Break Bread Together On Our Knees.""[7]

Bennett presents us with an intriguing conjecture with his passing comment that suggests blacks within the Episcopal Church contributed to the growing body of Afro-American religious folksong, to be known later as spirituals. Bennett seems to imply that the spiritual "Let Us Break Bread Together" originated among black Episcopalians possibly since the kneeling stance is assumed in communion and probably because the administering of the Holy Sacraments is central to Episcopal liturgy. Perhaps what is most intriguing about Bennett's hypothesis is that blacks other than those who were under the influence of the Methodists and Baptists were not to be excluded from certain musical practices that were popular among the masses of blacks. These musical practices included the singing of religious folk songs. Before the introduction of the organ in black Episcopal churches, which occurred in the 1820's, congregational singing made use of the performance practice known as "lining-out."

Most congregations, both black and white, developed what church authorities called "undesirable" practices in terms of congregational singing before the organ became the standard instrument for accompanying congregational singing. These "undesirable" practices consisted of the use of a highly embellished vocal line. The concerns of the clergy for improved congregational singing gave rise to singing schools, which were intended to promote the "regular" or "correct" way of singing as it was called, or "singing by note." The movement toward the establishment of singing schools began in New England in the eighteenth century, and by the second half of the century had become a regular institution in New England. St. Philip's (New York) established a church music school (to teach "singing by note") which held classes twice a week in the evenings, according to *Freedom's Journal*, October 26, 1827. There seemed to be no opposition to "singing by note" among black Episcopalians, at least not in New York City or Philadelphia; such was not the case in Philadelphia's Bethel A. M. E. church where the older people resisted vehemently to "singing by note." Among more enlightened black Episcopalians and black independents, the introduction of the choir and organ into the church service, as well as musical literacy, were viewed as *progressive* whereas the older communicants in the A. M. E. denomination regarded the *new practice* of music reading as having brought the devil into the church."[8]

An important musical activity to be noted among black Episcopalians during the early nineteenth century was church sponsored concerts. St.Philips (New York) was not only instrumental in establishing church music schools, but also led the way in sponsoring sacred concerts, usually consisting of large choral works often with orchestral accompaniment. Most often, the concerts featured the works of European composers, and occasionally the works of black composers were presented.[9]

There was a high performance standard placed on music in black congregations of the Church. Very often on the occasion of institutions and consecrations, clergy commented on the quality of singing. For example, Bishop Kemp, who consecrated St. James (Baltimore), made the following comments in recording the events of that day: " . . . the congregation was large and devout, . . . the responses were well made and the chanting and singing quite delightful."[10]

By the 1830's, the organ had become such a tradition at St. Thomas that when the Rev. J. M. Douglas accepted the call to St. Thomas, he described the church in the following way:

> "She stood alone in favor of education of ministry and people . . . and once spoken of in disparaging terms on account of care for cleanliness, decency in worship house, her carpeted aisles, her pews and *organ*, now closely imitated in all respects."[11]

Among Southern black communicants, it is not known whether communicants were actually able to read music. It is probable that they learned the chants and hymns by rote. However, in instances where singing was done without instrumental accompaniment, the singing was still commented upon as being "acceptable" and "well rendered." Probably, then, careful instruction was given in singing; probably, instruction was given in reading music as well as its performance.

It seems that music within black Episcopal Churches maintained its high quality during the 1840's. Most often, the quality of the music in black congregations was the subject of comment by clergy who visited these congregations. Such was the case at Christ Church, Providence, Rhode Island, which was admitted as a parish in June of 1843 and was originally led by Alexander Crummell. One of the white clergy who had charge of the parish submitted the following in his annual report:

> "This is the only colored church in New England, though there are several meeting-houses of different sects in the city of Providence. The services, the church and the worshippers, present an appearance of order, neatness and regularity which are seldom equated, and can hardly be surpassed. The organist is a colored girl under twenty years of age and the music is excellent."[12]

During the 1850's, church music among black Episcopalians continued to be given careful attention and thus was well performed, particularly since trained black musicians and composers were often Episcopalians. For example, at St. Philip's Church, Newark, which was instituted circa 1856, Peter P. O'Fake, a notable musician of Newark and a baritone, served as choir director beginning in 1856. Under O'Fake's leadership, the choir received favorable comments from the press.[13]

While Peter O'Fake was active in Newark, William Brady and Thomas J. Bowers, both black musicians, concertized in New York and Philadelphia during the 1850's. Little is known about William Brady, who died in 1854, except that he was a composer who James M. Trotter describes as a "composer of a musical service for the Episcopal Church." In addition to his musical activities in New York, Brady performed in Philadelphia from the 1820's through the early 50's. It has not been disclosed whether Brady was a musician in one of the black Episcopal Churches in New York City. However, it is likely that he was a musician at St. Philip's (New York) or at least an Episcopalian, as evidenced by his composing music for the Episcopal service.

Thomas J. Bowers, his brother John C. Bowers, and his sister, Sarah Sedgewick Bowers were prominent musicians in Philadelphia beginning in the 1850's and were members of St. Thomas, where their father was senior warden. St. Thomas has a distinctive history of musical activity beginning in the nineteenth century. Maude Cuney-Hare in *Negro Musicians and Their Music* (1936) mentions that much of the sacred music written about 1800 was composed for sevices at St. Thomas. Both Thomas Bowers and his brother, John served as organists at St. Thomas. The music historian James M. Trotter provides some informative insights into the Bowers family and sheds light on the quality of music in Philadelphia among the "elite," and by extension gives some idea of the quality of music at St. Thomas — at least during the period from the 1840's through the eighties:

> "The parents of the subject of this sketch [Thomas J. Bowers] although highly pleased with the natural musical qualities and with the accomplishments displayed by their children, were such strict church people as not to wish them to become public performers. Recognizing the pleasing, refining influence of music, they desired its practice by their children in the home-circle, for the most part; but were not adverse, however, to hearing its sweet and sacred strains issue from choir and organ in church service, not to having their children take part in the same."[14]

By the late 1850's, the use of the organ in worship among black Episcopalians had influenced black independent denominations to introduce instrumental music into their worship services as well. The following is an account of the influence that St. James (Baltimore) had on other black churches in that city, in terms of the introduction of the organ into the worship service:

> "This was a real novelty and invited strong denunciations from the colored churches of the city. Reproachful and sneering terms were applied to the church because of this introduction into the public services of the church the 'devil's music box.' Thus, the Church was an early witness for musical accessories in divine service, as well as for order and decorum in public worship. The indirect influence of St. James has been very great in this city, as the marvelous changes in the conduct of services in colored churches witnesseth."[15]

By the middle of the nineteenth century, black Episcopal churches in the North had thriving music programs. In the South on the plantations, musical practices among black Episcopalians tended to be within the folk tradition, that is, songs were sung unaccompanied.

The account of musical activities on a North Carolina plantation belonging to Ebenezer Pettigrew and Josiah Collins, which reported 100 black communicants, is probably representative of performance practices among southern black communicants. Bishop Ives, who worked among blacks on this North Carolina plantation, commented on "being struck by the beauty of the singing which is done without instrumental accompaniment."[16] Singing without instrumental accompaniment was also the case at Calvary Church in Charleston, South Carolina, where it was reported that "a choir of Negroes sang the chants and hymns without accompaniment;" this was on the occasion of the consecration of the building in 1849.[17]

Less wealthy parishes were not always able to purchase organs and thus sang without accompaniment. The oral tradition prevailed in parishes such as St. Paul's in Wilmington, North Carolina, which was organized in 1858; in North Carolina it was unlawful to teach reading to blacks, music was provided by "a choir of colored persons who were *orally* taught the catechism and to sing the psalms and hymns."[18]

Even when blacks were taught the hymns and psalms by note or by oral tradition, "undesirable performance practices" — as they were called by educated white and black clergy — did not seem to develop in black Episcopal churches as these "undesirable practices" developed in black independent churches.

The mode of worship among black Episcopalians became a distinctive feature of worship, so much so that a Swedish visitor to Cincinnati, Ohio, Frederika Bremer, made the following comments in a letter she sent to Sweden from Cincinnati, dated November 27, 1850:

> "I had in the forenoon visited a negro *Baptist church* belonging to the *Episcopal creed.* There were but few present, and they were of the negro [sic] aristocracy of the city. The mode of conducting the divine service was quiet, very proper, and a little tedious. The hymns were beautifully and exquisitely sung."[19]

With regard to the "undesirable practices" that developed in black independent churches, some black clergy such as Daniel Alexander Payne warned his A. M. E. congregation against "clapping and stamping feet in a ridiculous and heathenish way."[20] Such clergy as Payne seemed to associate demonstrative forms of religious expression with the "unenlightened."

Having been influenced by St. James (Baltimore) in introducing the organ into the church service, Payne mentions that the choir and organ were introduced in the Boston A. M. E. church in 1867. This event met with no opposition because, Payne says:

> "The membership of our Church in the enlightened city of Boston was so intelligent that they regarded the introduction of the choir and the organ as an advanced step in their religious public worship."[21]

By the close of the Civil War, a foundation had been laid in black Episcopal churches for church music that was rich and performed according to high standards. St. Thomas had led the way in this regard. By the mid-1860's, St. Thomas only owed a small balance on her organ, which was a significant achievement. And in the South, by the close of the War, school children were regularly drilled and given instruction in music and singing the chants.[22]

The Post-Bellum Period

Music in black Episcopal churches had become, by the post-bellum period, a "cultivated" or "genteel" tradition, as distinct from a "folk" or "vernacular" tradition.

Black Episcopal churches persisted in providing quality music in the worship service. The Rev. Calbraith B. Perry, a white cleric, worked in black congregations in Baltimore from the late 1860's through the late 70's. Having visited St. Philip's mission, established as a black congregation in 1868, Perry informs us that "it was a small structure but when the service began the small size of the mission was forgotten because of the sweet music." Perry goes on to add that "despite infrequent clergy leadership, the colored folks had loyalty and persistently maintained services."[23]

Even in small congregations, black Episcopalians apparently viewed the organ as a vital component of worship, so much so that at St. Philip's-St.Luke's (New Orleans), organized in 1878, a pipe organ was purchased in 1880 for a congregation of three men and ten women.[24]

Black Episcopal churches were most often noted in accounts of the musical activities of blacks in urban areas. St. Thomas (Chicago) is notable in this regard. The first rector of St. Thomas, the Rev. James E. Thompson, was apparently critical of the music there and likely guided its direction. St. Thomas (Chicago) was probably one of the churches to which the music historian James M. Trotter refers in discussing the music situation in black churches in Chicago in the 1870's:

> "Besides several fine church-choirs, there is a large organization of well-trained vocalists, the performance of which have been highly spoken of by journals of Chicago . . . ."[25]

It is also interesting to note that all three of Thompson's children were musicians. (One son, J. DeKoven Thompson, composed a song, which was sung at the funeral of President William McKinley.)[26]

While black Episcopalians primarily sang hymns from the Anglican tradition, in at least one instance sources indicate that Methodist hymns were sung by black Episcopalians. This was an interesting development. And perhaps the most illuminating discussion in this regard is offered by Calbraith B. Perry in his book, *Twelve Years Among the Colored People* (1884) in which we are provided with a glimpse of the musical activities at St. Mary's Chapel, (Baltimore) established in 1878. Perry writes that "a choral service was regularly held on Friday nights and also at 4 p.m. on Sundays after the close of the Sunday School session when people gathered for short musical services."[27]

Perry's descriptions about musical life at St. Mary's indicate that at least one black Episcopal church had been influenced by Methodist hymnody. The hymns that are mentioned were, as Perry indicates, "familiar hymns" to the congregation of black Episcopalians. In describing the evening service held at eight o'clock — a shortened form of evening prayer — Perry says that "the chants were sung" and "the hymns were set to inspiriting tunes which were interspersed with familiar Methodist hymns: 'Coronation,' 'There is a Fountain,' and 'Nearer My God to Thee.'"[28]

These comments of Perry's are revealing for two reasons: it is likely that the musical practices among black Methodists, at least in the city of Baltimore, had affected Episcopalians; and it is not too farfetched to conclude that the hymn tradition among blacks was interdenominational, as it continues to be.

Musical people in Baltimore during the 1880's "worthy of mention," include certain choir members of St. Mary's Episcopal Church:

> "Mr. H. C. Bishop, general director; Mr. W. H. Bishop, precentor; J. Hopkins Johns, who has a very pleasing voice; Mr. J. Taylor, a fine basso, who has been a member of a meritorious concert-troupe; Mr. C. A. Johnson, organist; and Mr. George Barrett, tenor."[29]

The music historian Trotter goes on to add that C. A. Johnson, the organist, has on "several occasions been the director of excellent public concerts in Baltimore and its vicinity, and is deserving of much praise for his activity in promoting the music-loving spirit. The same may be said of Mr. George Barrett, another member of St. Mary's Choir."[30] C. A. Johnson was also the leader of an association of musicians called "the Monumental Cornet

Band," which furnished instrumental music for festive occasions at St. Mary's and in the city of Baltimore.[31] It should be noted that St. Mary's choir members, the organist at the Bethel Methodist Church, and members of the Sharp-Street Church choir were apparently the most musical Afro-Americans in Baltimore at that time. The point is that during the 1880's, music at St. Mary's was more noteworthy than the music at St. James if Trotter's comments are an actual account of the musical situation in Baltimore at that time.

The musical legacy of St. Mary's (Baltimore) was maintained by the Rev. Hutchens C. Bishop, who was the fourth rector of St. Philips (New York) and whose older brothers and sisters were among the pioneers of St. James (Baltimore). Bishop established the second congregation in Baltimore, St. Mary's. Bishop was confirmed at St. Mary's and sang in the choir there. Upon his coming to St. Philip's (New York), Bishop was attentive to the music performed, given his nurturing and the musical activities in which he engaged as a youth.[32] The men and boys choir at St. Philip's became a recognized concert group under Bishop's rectorship.

Bishop's interest in music extended beyond the church. He was a member of the board of directors of the Negro Music School Settlement (New York City).

It was not unusual for black Episcopal churches to spawn musicians of note and most often these musicians were formally trained. For example, there was Mrs. Arianna Cooley Sparrow who was a member of the Handel and Haydn Society in Boston during the 1880's, and who because of "excellent training retained the natural sweetness of her voice and purity of tone that enabled her to sing acceptably in St. Augustine Episcopal Church (Boston) when over eighty years of age."[33]

By the 1890's, we know for certain that women had been admitted to church choirs. At St. Matthew's (Detroit), where women were admitted to the choir in 1892, they were not allowed in the choir stalls but had to occupy the front pews.[34] (Women, however, had historically served as organists in black Episcopal churches.)

By the turn of the century, black Episcopal churches were still recognized for their music. Writing in 1897 about black life in Philadelphia, W. E. B. DuBois discusses various black Episcopal churches in that city and goes on to add that the Church of the Crucifixion (which was over fifty years old in 1897) was "perhaps the most effective church in the city for its benevolent and rescue work and it makes especial feature of good music with its vested choir."[35]

In a history of St. Philip's by the Rev. B. F. DeCosta, published in 1889, we are informed that "for the benefit of those who never enjoyed literary privileges, it was the custom, as in many churches *long before*, and *even afterwards*, to line off the psalms and hymns, in order that all might join in the praise of the Almighty God."[36]

The aforementioned quote by the Rev. DeCosta is important for several reasons. Although DeCosta's comments are about a specific black congregation, by extension we perhaps are provided with some idea about the extent of musical practices in black Episcopal congregations during the late nineteenth and early twentieth centuries. Contrary to the commonly held notion that all black Episcopalians were literate, we know from DeCosta's comments that this was not entirely the case, at least not by the beginning of this century. From DeCosta's insights, we can conclude that an oral musical tradition persisted to a degree in black Episcopal churches into the twentieth century.

From the turn of the century through the early twenties several events are worth mentioning that directly or indirectly influenced music in black Episcopal Churches. For instance, by 1910, St. Athanasius School, an Episcopal Church School for blacks, was founded which started as a mission in 1884 and developed into a high and training school; among its "efficient department" were domestic science, manual training and *music*.[37]

Sources disclose that it was not uncommon for priests to be trained musicians in the early twentieth century. For instance, at St. Augustine's (Atlantic City), which was spawned by St. James (Baltimore), there was the Rev. James Nelson Denver, the vicar whom Bragg describes as "having a fair high school education," and "a musician and a general 'hustler'."[38] The Rev. Maximo Duty, vicar of St. Philip's (Richmond) from 1901 to 1903, was also a musician, while the Rev. Issac A. McDonald, rector of St. Philip's from 1938 to 1942, served also as the choir director.[39]

A "cultivated" musical tradition characterized black Episcopal churches in urban areas by the early twentieth century — except in some instances where the psalms and hymns were still "lined-out." It has been reported that at a mission in Burroughs, Georgia, communicants employed the practice of "lining out" during the early twentieth century.[40]

The Contemporary Scene

Church sponsored concerts that began in the 1820's and continued full swing into the twentieth century in black Episcopal churches had always provided performance outlets for black musicians. Marian Anderson gave her first Detroit concert on November 1, 1926 at St. Matthew's Church to raise funds for the rectory.[41]

In the twentieth century, black congregations of the Church also produced musicians of note. This continued a tradition that had been set in motion during the nineteenth century. For instance Carl R. Diton (1886-1969), composer and teacher, served as organist at St. Thomas (Philadelphia) during the 1920's. Diton is famous for his organ fantasy, based on the spiritual, "Swing Low, Sweet Chariot." He is also well known for his choral arrangements of Afro-American spirituals. Melville Charlton, who was born in New York in 1883, was perhaps the leading organist of the black race at that time and was the first black to become a member of the prestigious American Guild of Organists. He was organist at St. Philip's Episcopal Church (New York).[42]

An interesting musical activity developed during the 1930's at St. Ambrose (New York), under the rectorship of the Rev. E. E. Durant. Durant, a West Indian, was concerned that services were "bright and that people entered heartily into singing," and held contests to promote congregational singing. One such contest involved the singing of six hymns; the competition occurred between the men and the women and between the congregation and the choir. Durant was so concerned about the quality of music at St. Ambrose that he always attended all choir rehearsals when he was in the city. About Episcopal churches, he says: "Some people complain about the dullness of some churches, all people like a bright spirited service. I love it myself."[43]

St. Ambrose, under Durant's leadership, spawned at least one musician, an organist of note. Clarence E. Whiteman, presently professor of organ and theory at Virginia State College, served as an acolyte at St. Ambrose and credits this exposure and experience as having influenced his becoming an organist. Whiteman's formal musical education includes degrees from Manhattan School of Music, Guilmant Organ School and the School of Sacred Music, formerly at the Union Theological Seminary (presently at Yale Divinity School), and from Trinity College in London. He served as organist and choir master at St. Philip's (New York) where in 1973, for regular worship, he featured music composed by blacks.[44]

By the 1960's, the state of congregational singing in many black Episcopal churches was critical. It is likely that the comments given in the parish profile of St. Philip's (Richmond) are representative of the state of music within black Episcopal parishes: "The congregation is passive in participating in the service, both in singing and in prayer response."

Presently, there is real effort underway to revitalize and rejuvenate the worship experience among black Episcopalians. Much of this effort involves the appropriation of traditional materials from the Afro-American experience to the Episcopal liturgy. Perhaps the Rev. Arthur Myron Cochran led the way in his arrangements of music (largely based on Afro-American spirituals) for the Communion Service which were published in 1925 and revived by the St. Augustine's College Choir in a recording of the Cochran Mass, produced by the Rev. Robert B. Hunter (presently rector of Church of the Atonement, Washington, D. C.)

Making the liturgy relevant to contemporary society and to the Afro-American experience was largely undertaken in the ministry of the late Rev. Lee Benefe and continues in the ministry of the Rev. Kwasi (Anthony) Thornhill, formerly director of the Alexander Crummell Center for Worship and Learning in Detroit, among many others.

The Rev. Thornhill is concerned about the relationship of Word, music and Mass and maintains that "the key to bringing Episcopalians together is to break down the separateness between the choir, the congregation and the minister. The Word, the music and the Mass must move toward wholeness . . . . This is achieved in several ways: by altering the Mass into contemporary language, and by experimenting with spatial relationships in terms of the choir, congregation and the minister and passing from a strictly hymnbook tradition to one which is oral in the sense that the music and text become so familiar that people are able to enter into the worship experience without being bound to the printed page."[45] The oral tradition about which Thornhill speaks characterizes the religious song tradition of Afro-Americans. And Afro-Americans have historically employed the oral tradition, even in singing hymns written and composed by non-blacks.

Mainline denominations have begun to recognize the power of black song and black worship style and are finding ways of utilizing this music, i.e. Afro-American music, within the framework of their liturgies. Such a movement is underway in the Episcopal church. For example, the Rev. Wm. James Walker, a black priest, commissioned Lena McLin, an Afro-American who is a music director and a composer, to compose a Mass for the Episcopal liturgy in which one can not help but note the Afro-Americanisms in the compositional style. Also at the 1974 meeting of the Union of Black Episcopalians, the music used for the Mass was in the contemporary Afro-American religious music idiom referred to as "gospel." More recently the Office of Black Ministries of the Episcopal Church has undertaken a project of which this essay is a part. This project, a hymnal, calls attention to Afro-American religious songs and other hymns that have been popular among Afro-Americans.

Summary

The activities — music being one — of blacks in the Episcopal church need further documentation. This of course is a challenge to scholars.

This essay will hopefully provoke more study and research of the musical activities of black Episcopalians. In the course of this essay, attention was given to highlighting these activities and in an indirect way topics for future research were illuminated. What are some of the questions that have been raised from this discussion? For this writer, several. For instance, what are the possibilities of an Episcopal source for the Afro-American spiritual, "Let Us Break Bread Together on Our Knees"? Or to what extent were the religious folk songs of Afro-Americans used in black parishes with black or white leadership? How were these songs performed? Another question that comes to mind is: what are the cultural and social factors that gave rise to music making among black Episcopalians? These examples must suffice.

I hope this essay demonstrates the validity of the study of the music of blacks in the Episcopal church and demonstrates that further study of this area is imperative to the history of church music.

[1]Gilbert Chase, *America's Music,* New York: McGraw-Hill, 1966, 236-37, quoting Henry Russell, *Cheer Boys Cheer,* n.p., n.d., 84-85.

[2]William Douglas, *Annals of the First African Church,* Philadelphia: Kerg and Baird, 1862, 54, (my italics).

[3]Edgar E. Pennington, *Thomas Bray's Associates and Their Work Among the Negroes,* Worchester, Mass.: American Antiquarian Society, 1939, 25 quoting S. P. G. Series A, V. #49 (October 20, 1709); see also Denzie T. Clifton, "Anglicanism and Negro Slavery in Colonial America," *Historical Magazine of the Protestant Episcopal Church* XXXIX (March 1970), 63-64.

[4]Pennington, *Thomas Bray's . . . ,*78.

[5]Ibid., 17 quoting the "Minutes of the Meetings of the P. P. G. (1729-1735)," 62-65; (my italics).

[6]Ibid., 82 quoting *S. P. G. Series B,* XIII, #219 and *S. P. G. Series* B, XIX #68.

[7]Robert A. Bennett, "Black Episcoplians: A History from the Colonial Period to the Present Day," *Historical Magazine of the Protestant Episcopal Church,* XLIII (September 1974), 239.

[8]Daniel Alexander Payne, *History of the A. M. E. Church,* Nashville, Tenn.: Publishing House of the A. M. E. Sunday School Union, 1891, 452-453; D. A. Payne, *Recollections of Seventy Years (*Nashville, Tenn.) 1888, 234.

[9]Eileen Southern, "Musical Practices in Black Churches . . . ," *Journal of American Musicological Society* XXX (Summer 1977), 306, quoting from the concert program as it appeared in *Freedom's Journal,* September 23, 1827.

[10]George F. Bragg, *First Negro Priest on Southern Soil,* Baltimore: Church Advocate Press, 1909, 13.

[11]Douglas, *Annals,* 130; (my italics).

[12]George D. Bragg, *History of the Afro-American Group of the Episcopal Church,* Baltimore: Church Advocate Press, 1922, 102-103 quoting the *A. M. E. Magazine,* 1845.

[13]Eileen Southern, *Music of Black Americans,* New York: W. W. Norton and Co., 1971, 122. James M. Trotter, *Music and Some Highly Musical People*, Boston: Lee and Shepherd, 1880 (reprint Chicago: Afro-American Press, 1969), 306. O'Fake also had the distinction of being the first black to conduct the Newark Theatre Orchestra.

[14]Trotter, 132.

[15]Bragg, *First Priest . . . ,*30.

[16]John Hope Franklin, "Negro Episcopalians in Ante-Bellum North Carolina," *Historical Magazine of the Protestant Episcopal Church,* XIII/3 (September 1944), 221 quoting the *Journal of the North Carolina Convention*, 1843, 13.

[17]Robert F. Durden, "The Establishment of Cavalry Church," Charleston: Dalcho Historical Society, 1965, 82 quoting *The Charleston Gospel Messenger and The Protestant Episcopal Register*, XIX (1852), 215-216.

[18]Allen J. Jackson, *100th Anniversary Bulletin of St. Marks Wilmington 1975*, quoting *The Church Messenger* (Winston, North Carolina) July 21, 1881. St. Paul's was a mission of St. Marks which was consecrated on June 18, 1975, (my italics).

[19]Quoted in Eileen Southern, *Readings in Black American Music*, New York: W. W. Norton & Co., 1971, 112-113 (my italics).

[20]Ibid., 26-64; 68-70.

[21]Payne, *History of the A. M. E. Church*, 458.

[22]George F. Bragg, *The Story of Old St. Stephens*, Petersburg, Va., Baltimore: Church Advocate Print, n. d.; Allen E. Jackson, *100th Anniversary Bulletin St. Marks*, Wilmington, N. C.

[23]Calbraith B. Perry, *Twelve Years Among the Colored People*, New York: James Patt and Co., 1884, 22.

[24]Rev. Herman Cope Duncan, *History of the Diocese of Louisiana*, New Orleans: A. W. Hyatt, 1883, 227-228.

[25]Trotter, *Music and Some Highly Musical People*, 321.

[26]*The Thirty-Six Anniversary Tea Program Bulletin* (St. Thomas, Chicago) Sunday, June 18, 1884; Maude Cuney-Hare, *Negro Musicians and Their Music,* Washington, D. C.: Associated Publisher, 1936, 227.

[27]Perry, *Twelve Years . . .* , 75.

[28]Ibid., 78.

[29]Trotter, 329.

[30]Ibid.

[31]Perry, 78.

[32]Bragg, *Afro-American Group . . .* , 88; Shelton Bishop, "A History of St. Philip's Church," *Historical Magazine of the Protestant Episcopal Church* XII (March 1946), 298-317.

[33]Maude Cuney-Hare, *Negro Musicians and Their Music,* 221.

[34]From *Centennial Celebration Bulletin 1846-1946,* St. Matthew's Episcopal Church, Detroit.

[35]W. E. B. DuBois, *The Philadelphia Negro*, New York: Schocken Books, 1899, 217.

[36]The Rev. B. F. DeCosta, *Three Score and Ten: the Story of the St. Philip's Church New York City,* New York: printed for the parish, 1889, 15; (my italics).

[37]Bragg, *Afro-American Group*, 222.

[38]Ibid., 174.

[39]"Parish Profile," St. Philip's Episcopal Church, Richmond, Va., October 1975 unpublished MS.

[40]Personal interview, Dr. Tollie Caution, April 1978, New York City.

[41]*Centennial Celebration Bulletin*, 1846-1946, St. Matthew's Episcopal Church.

[42]Maude Cuney-Hare, 340-341.

[43]Rev. E. Ellio Durant, *The Romance of an Ecclesiastical Adventure*, n. p., n. d. (1946?).

[44]Eileen Southern, "Conversation With . . . Clarence E. Whiteman, Organ-Music Collector," *Black Perspective in Music*, Fall 1978, 168-187.

[45]Personal interview, Rev. Kwasi Thornhill, New York City, March, 1978.

Alphabetical Index of Titles and *First Lines*